Options Trading

Stress Free Crash Course

How to earn money weekly with latest strategies in the market- Beginners tips to income your profit in Day Trading- Swing Trading- Forex- Option Trading

By

RICHARD GAIN

© **Copyright 2020 by (RICHARD GAIN) - All rights reserved.**

This document is geared towards providing exact and reliable information in regards to the topic and issue covered. The publication is sold with the idea that the publisher is not required to render accounting, officially permitted, or otherwise, qualified services. If advice is necessary, legal or professional, a practiced individual in the profession should be ordered.

- From a Declaration of Principles which was accepted and approved equally by a Committee of the American Bar Association and a Committee of Publishers and Associations.

In no way is it legal to reproduce, duplicate, or transmit any part of this document in either electronic means or in printed format. Recording of this publication is strictly prohibited and any storage of this document is not allowed unless with written permission from the publisher. All rights reserved.

The information provided herein is stated to be truthful and consistent, in that any liability, in terms of inattention or otherwise, by any usage or abuse of any policies, processes, or directions contained within is the solitary and utter responsibility of the recipient reader. Under no circumstances will any legal responsibility or blame be held against the publisher for any reparation, damages, or monetary loss due to the information herein, either directly or indirectly.

Respective authors own all copyrights not held by the publisher.

The information herein is offered for informational purposes solely, and is universal as so. The presentation of the information is without contract or any type of guarantee assurance.

The trademarks that are used are without any consent, and the publication of the trademark is without permission or backing by the trademark owner.

All trademarks and brands within this book are for clarifying purposes only and are the owned by the owners themselves, not affiliated with this document.

Disclaimer

Trading of futures, bonds, and options entails a substantial risk of failure and is not ideal for any investor. Futures, stocks, and options value may fluctuate, and as a consequence, consumers may risk more than their initial investment. The impact of seasonal and geopolitical events on market prices is already factored in. The heavily leveraged nature of markets means that small market movements will have a big impact on your trading account, and it can also go against you, resulting in large losses or can work for you, resulting in large gains.

If the market moves against you, you may be able to sustain a total loss in excess of the amount that you deposited. You are liable for both the threats and financial services you use, and the trading method you have selected. You should not work as a trader unless you completely understand the nature of the work you are going into and the extent of your exposure to loss.

All trading techniques are deployed at your own risk.

Table Of Content

INTRODUCTION 8

CHAPTER 1: INTRODUCTION TO OPTIONS 11

1.1 Trading benefits with options trading 17

1.2 The Leverage Inherent in Options 18

1.3 Playing the Downside with Options 19

1.4 Risk control and the different options approaches 20

1.5 Take advantage of Options in Certain Circumstances 21

1.6 Using Options for Insurance 21

1.7 A Trader's Positive Attitude or winning mindset 23

CHAPTER 2: SPREAD TRADING 32

2.1 Spread Trading Overview 32

2.2 Directional Trading Vs. Spread Trading 35

2.3 Greed and Fear 35

2.4 Swing trading 35

CHAPTER 3: USING CALL OPTION FOR INCOME AND SPECULATION 45

3.1 The Long Call Strategy — Using Calls for Speculation 47

3.2 The Bull Call Spread — An Alternative to the Long Call Strategy 50

3.3 The Covered Call — Generating Additional Income from Your Stock Portfolio 52

3.4 Long-Term Speculation — The Special Case of LEAPS 57

3.5 The Bear Call Spread — Collecting Income from Option Selling........ 58

3.6 A Word on Risk Management... 60

CHAPTER 4: USING PUTS FOR SPECULATION, PROTECTION AND INCOME.. 61

4.1 The Long-Put Plan-The Downside Play 61

4.2 The Bear Put Spread — Speculating of spreads to the downside 65

4.3 Income Generation-Selling Naked Puts 66

4.4 Utilizing long put to secure the assets 69

CHAPTER 5: TECHNICAL AND FUNDAMENTAL ANALYSIS BASICS 74

CHAPTER 6: MODIFIED AND ADVANCED CONCEPT STRATEGIES.. 87

6.1 Options of pricing — What is a "fair" cost for such an option?.......... 88

6.2 Understanding Volatility-Critical Value for Traders in Options 91

6.3 Time ranges — Mixing options with various expiry dates................. 94

6.4 Spreading the Percentage — Purchasing and trading unequal options 96

6.5 Combining Calls and Puts in a Single Strategy 98

6.6 Buying stock with Covered Combine inexpensively 101

6.7 Trade in the Collar: Hedging the portfolio for so little to more 103

CHAPTER 7: LINKS AND STEPS TO ACTIVATE WITH YOUR BROKER 106

CHAPTER 8: CAPITAL SAVING AND RULES FOR OPTION TRADING 125

8.1 Index Options – A valuable investment manager tool 125

8.2 Use Index Options to securing your portfolio 127

8.3 Use Index Options for Diversification and Speculation 128

CHAPTER 9: COMMON MISTAKES TO AVOID AND SUGGESTIONS 131

CHAPTER 10: LEAPS STRATEGY TO WIN THE GREAT REWARD 141

CHAPTER 11: LOW AND HIGH VOLATILITY TRADING ENVIRONMENTS 145

11.1 Increased volatility 146

11.2 High Turnover Profits 152

CHAPTER 12: SET THE PASSIVE PROFITS BY TRADING OPTIONS 156

CHAPTER 13: OPTIONS CASE STUDY- RELATIONSHIP BETWEEN UNDERLYING ASSETS AND OPTIONS 162

CHAPTER 14: GREEKS METHOD 166

CHAPTER 15: OTHER IMPORTANT FACTORS FOR OPTIONS 170

CONCLUSION 179

REFERENCES 183

Introduction

Options offer enormous incentives for someone that is unsure of how the capital market would behave in the short future – and this covers almost any stockholder. They help you to optimize your equity resources, offer you more versatility while considering financial decisions, and empower you to customize your risk to suit your individual comfort level. In brief, options could be used successfully for a variety of different reasons, such as the 3 main ones that we will discuss throughout this book which include using them: (1) speculating on the benefits sector, (2) earning income and boosting your return on investment, and (3) protecting against a sudden downturn in the valuation of a stock, or hedging your whole portfolio against sector danger.

In the early nineties, the dot.com trend proved the simplicity with which profit is made in a volatile market. However, it is another side to the equation as well, as the consequence of the trend has shown. You can blot out the paper gains and suffer huge losses in the apparent matter of seconds.

Most people have learned through their observations since the slump of the sector that stock market buying is quite fickle, there is a great deal of risk of investing, that one needs to purchase and trade at the right moment and that taking the required choices is always overcome by anxiety. Such risks have left them afraid of the financial markets while in the same period have a tendency to manipulate the business to boost their personal financial status.

This combination of passions, the urge to invest in collaboration with the apprehension of declines, is sometimes exacerbated by misunderstandings regarding financial markets. For starters, most people are going to have it as granted that only if market values increase will the money be created. But believe this or not, it would've been false! What will you do if they asked you that?

Is it a method to safeguard what you invested in? How if you'd been informed you might?

Cover stocks in which you've spent your entire savings? Are you concerned?

Training how and when to preserve your capital no matter if the market goes, even though the stock value dropped?

How is it if you have been informed, you can produce capital on stocks that you already own every weekend? You wouldn't have to sit patiently for equity values to increase, but you may produce cash on a constructive basis each month. Will you be curious to learn?

How will that be done? The overarching purpose of this guide is to illustrate how, depending on the way it travels, one can prosper throughout the market and when to do that with dispassion and a strong sense of social security.

This book offers you with both the requisite strategy to obtain that aim through spreads trading strategies. Combined with a knowledge of stock analysis approaches and technologies with the purpose of defining their probable potential for future moves, this awareness should allow users to trade in any sector efficiently and continuously.

These topics and other relevant concerns are explored in-depth in this text, as are recommendations as to how exactly one can switch from a knowledge of skills required to successfully trade in the global marketplace.

The suggested approaches have been carefully checked, and strict obedience to them will give you techniques for gaining inventory & options. Over time they will produce strong and stable returns combined with enormous personal gratification.

Chapter 1: Introduction to options

How is it that the options are much wrongheaded as a threat and risk minefield? What can we make good sense of it and stare at options as instruments to limit our dangers, enhance our profits, and simultaneously see what we are doing? That's the nature of the Easy choice and this book — how to make something apparently complicated quick.

Options were increasingly common, notably in the United States. Apart from being limited exclusively to banks and skilled fund managers, selling options is now commonplace across all walks of existence for "retail" traders. Nevertheless, in some areas, the definition of choices is often viewed with uncertainty and trepidation. A friend cautioned me of what I was heading into when I first started on meaningful trading, but trading may be as secure unless you have it to be.

The basic reality is you must have a workable business plan. It needs to maintain your risk low and high your reward potential. You want to have a system and cleanness in your plan so that you can always follow it. My options strategy trading has risen tremendously simpler over the years.

It helps grow the following characteristics — and these could all be built to make it a dealer.

Requirements for the profitable venture in patience Perseverance knowledge

- Honesty
- Pre-planning
- Discipline
- Knowledge
- Patience
- perseverance

Perseverance

Keep tight. If you trust in anything, you will commit to it before you accomplish your target. And then set another objective until you have achieved your aim.

Having started on the task of being a good trader, to get there, you have to stick to it. Anybody should do it. I have witnessed that with my learner's time after time again, where the most unexpected characters can become incredible traders — including those

who don't believe they will?

Give oneself manageable targets in a reasonable time period, to be rational. So, you'll be thoroughly acquainted with the 4 major risk profiles of choices by next week. It's likely you will do something overnight. Keep establishing targets that are attainable (but find them a minor challenge), so you can keep up the excitement of training and acquiring knowledge. You will also continue building their trust as you walk along, comforting oneself of your capacity to comprehend anything that you put your heart to. This guide should help you develop your faith, as it is a straightforward book and simple to read and learn. So, just keep riding and appreciate the accumulation cycle.

Patience

Among the most thrilling things, you would have in the working life is earning good money throughout the stocks. I did it in 2 types, allowing improvements of hundreds of proportions every period. Maybe the 1st one was more chance than a decision. It was also by the use of skills that took some moments to build. Take a moment to determine your plan and develop your talents. A time arrives where you just feel part of the great economy and commerce while you are presented with its most visible openings. When you can turn down under standard chances with a shoulder shrug, you'll know you've come in.

Trust your instincts, if you are fresh to all this. Look at this method: already, after one lesson, would you recognize yourself willing to do major surgery? Oh, the same goes for stocks, and more so for selling options. Treat yourselves with learning. You are going to start experiencing this by studying this novel, offering yourselves a learning experience. If you already know stocks, then it is the first move. And just when you first had to be familiar with exchanging securities, you now have to be confident with trading futures, too.

In fact, if you're confident enough to deal, you'll need the flexibility to do the exchange itself. We've always had the feeling of moving so early into an undertaking even if we weren't fully sure this was the best idea to do. Be careful, breathe deeply if you need to, and still stick with your trade schedule.

Last but not least, compassion also includes picking a market segment where moment works in someone's pursuit or where their disadvantage is coated. There are lots of approaches in this guide to you to pick from; however, you should still try to keep it easy. Whatever one you end up choosing, every time wait to get the right chance to offer yourself. I hold to a few chart trends to sell, so if they don't turn up, I don't have to exchange. Qualified professional professionals make the success of the capital. So, invest heavily in what you are commercializing.

Be calm about your attraction towards acquiring money. The calmer you are thus, the stronger it will be for you. This is not to lay quietly and do. None — this is complacency, not caution. Offer yourselves time to study, acquire knowledge, and eventually start regularly practicing what you're learning so you can begin a cycle of getting profit and creating wealth.

In accordance with the practice of persistence, the idea of accruing is adopted. If you can earn only 1 % per week, that would imply greater than 67 five percent in just 1 year, a streak that would be insanely jealous of any money manager. If you begin only with $10,000 in the account, the given figure describes the compounding power:

Weekly return %	Monthly return %	1 year	2 years	3 years	3-year return %
1%	4%	$16,777	$28,146	$47,220	472%
2%	8.24%	$28,003	$78,418	$219,597	2,196%
3%	12.55%	$46,509	$216,307	$1,006,021	10,060%
4%	16.99%	$76,866	$590,836	$4,541,517	45,415%
5%	21.55%	$126,428	$1,598,406	$20,208,201	202,083%

This panel will be here to advise you on the need for caution. Generate your gains, then let the compounding do the job for you.

Knowledge

Having acquired the need for courage for both knowledge acquisition and self-trading, let us note that understanding is now attainable with such speed and ease that this is eminently attainable in a relatively swift period. Tools now exist to visualize the trading history, so there are numerous papers and websites intended to help build your database of knowledge.

The best knowledge is derived from experience. To say, "Trade mechanically" is all very well, but few of them do.

Feelings are a component of our beings, so it is more productive to operate around them rather than dismiss them. That's all about my trading plan — staying safe and still being capable of playing for the huge victories. Remember that training is based on experience. We can all recall our school teachers most seriously, correct? You can remember the funniest, most terrifying, the dirtiest, the loveliest, and the nastiest, but I'm going to bet you have a hard time remembering something about the lecturers who were in the middle somewhere — those of us who barely had a conceptual effect on you in decades of being in that class.

The same holds true for trade. A lot of education able to trade is based on experience. The most relevant form of studying trading, in fact, is based on experience. It is by the intense interactions where you find out more about oneself in both good and bad times. Most genius traders encountered terrible things, but, crucially, they stepped back to the counter and implemented what they knew. I earned a lot of money really easily; I felt I was invincible and then immediately gave back some of it. Trust me, I wasn't feeling too confident about this, but I knew. What is more, I implemented the tutorials.

Honesty

If you want to grow into a good investor or trader, you must be realistic with yourselves. Your outcomes ultimately determine just how nice you are. Their actions are the duty, not that of anybody else. Trying to blame others never tends to help. If you're pushing the lever, then you're in charge.

Pre-planning

Your every trade must be pre-planned. With this, you have to know your

- Breakeven points
- Potential danger

- Potential gain

You do have to prepare:

- Your access controls
- Your exit point, if it is to ...
- Take benefit or
- Stop losses with trading options,

I prefer to base every stop-loss mostly on the company's securities. The company's asset is usually more volatile than any of its options, thereby making it easy to make the loss-cutting choice depending on market price, potential, and whatever the fundamental commodity is. The first element of planning and preparation is to pick the common assets itself owing to the design of the chart. You then build the business strategy, which includes,

Discipline — The Key to Success

When you've had the perseverance to obtain the experience and implement the core values discussed earlier, it's vitally important not to spend everything. You have to be rigorously controlled and enforce the control every time. It means

You always do the pre-planning.

- You use the experience of yourself (and others too).
- You are not deviating from the reasonable strategy you have suggested.

You are making the first measures to be more meticulous in that sense. The practice is essential to business. And the most complex of trading networks cannot work without managing money.

By rigorously adhering to sound credit-management values, you make sure if your loss is reduced and that your earnings can run.

1.1 Trading benefits with options trading

A major advantage choice over other trading instruments is that either an up- or down-market choice investor will profit. You think that when you purchase an option, the corresponding stock can shift in the path you wish. If you are right, then you're making a return. If you're incorrect, then you're losing revenue. But it's just about 2 factors: Time — because at some stage the contract right still ends, and scheduling. Timing is a major key for options trading and is compatible with other types of investing.

This guide aims to show how you can help meet your investing ambitions by incorporating options for your investing arsenal. How you use choices relies on what you plan to do and how much chance you can tolerate taking. Many investors believe in options mostly as speculation and stand-alone offer. And this is certainly how they will be found. Potential applications of choices, though, go well beyond mere speculation — as we'll aim to illustrate in the novel.

This research will address a variety of alternative approaches that demonstrate how flexible alternatives are to help you meet your financial stake objectives while managing your risk as well. Whether you choose to cover long equity positions, reduce your inventory, maximize cash, or guarantee gains from paper — there is an option approach to benefit you. If you choose to eliminate as much value as possible, there are several rather conservative approaches that will help you to control risk while still through portfolio earnings. Just as a skilled chess expert perceives the board as a whole and may not target strategies on a single piece of movement, a really well-informed entrepreneur can incorporate alternatives into a greater investment strategy.

1.2 The Leverage Inherent in Options

Every contract option offers you the opportunity to purchase (a put option) or offer (a call option) 100 stock shares at a given price (the margin requirement) by a certain time period (the expiry date). When you purchase an option, you're hoping the stock can push in the path you've expected and fast normally enough to make a profit. The cost of an option — the premium option — is far inferior to the price of purchasing 100 stock shares. For e.g., purchasing 100 stock shares presently worth $60 a share will cost $6000. If the premium price on this stock on a call option is $4, you will pay just $400 for that contract. That grants you the opportunity to purchase 100 stock shares-but you don't have to. Which $400 gives you $6,000 shares of assets to control. This is leverage.

When you buy a place, you get a particular form of leverage. A put option grants you the opportunity to offer 100 stock options, so you don't need to buy the money. The investor held expects the stock price will go down. The put will become more valuable if it does and can be sold at a profit.

Buying puts or calls as mere betting offers you the opportunity to make money on price change, but without needing to shell out huge money at considerable expense. The main danger when you buy equity securities is that now the value will plummet. So, if you buy stock $6,000 in 100 stock shares and its market price drops to $30, then you lose $3,000. However, if you purchase a $4 premium call alternative, the worst, you'll ever risk $400. And when you're holding the same 100 common options, there's just a time frame of the amount at stake.

Using options throughout this way obviously often entails danger. The value of the right will decrease if the market price will not shift in the way you expected. And if the market price isn't rising at all, time is acting against you. An ever-looming expiry date ensures that the interest drops out of the day-to-day product, and you will sacrifice the total price you charged for the product. And even though leveraging is attractive, a certain level of danger comes with it.

1.3 Playing the Downside with Options

Most equity investors just consider a bullish viewpoint. But as history has demonstrated, average market values will fall over lengthy stretches. Owning stock can be a costly experience when this occurs. Going long the money, however, should not be the only method to participate in the equity market. If you believe a stock is going to go down, you can sell a short stock.

Forex stock may be a dangerous undertaking. You assume the valuation would decline as you shorten a stock, so if you are correct, then you will close the short place at a benefit. Small investors launch the place by borrowing their broker's stock at a reasonable rate of interest and then attempting to sell it to the market. They buy back the stock and shut the position — the reverse of the conventional purchase-then-sell formula any stockholder recognizes. The risk of short-sellers is their timing is right, and the stock's market value is rising. If this happens — it may lead to massive damages that are potentially infinite. That is a very dangerous game to play — and for most investors, short selling might not be a suitable strategy.

Placing options instead of inventory to play down demand, however, offers the same incentive with less risk. Once you purchase puts if the value of the implied vol declines, you make a return. And placing investing on a down market may be profitable — assuming that timing is correct. In the same period, the exposure is restricted to the prime paying rate.

1.4 Risk control and the different options approaches

You monitor how much chance you have with the choices. You can purchase one or more of those products. You're not inherently at the discretion of a gullible market that has terrible consequences that can make and break a strategy. You will control the exposure by just bringing in as many as you want to open to possible failure.

The biggest advantage investors have here is how they can continue to sit the market out. And if a stock drops half its worth, the equity holder will only carry on receiving dividends as well as look for the price to follow the opposite course. Although the buyer choice will face less danger, they do have less time. Although certain alternatives, such as Jumps, can have a week or two before expiry, most alternatives just last a few weeks. If you ever don't make the income until expiry, you're just failing. That's why it's so important to have certain basic education options — to get acquainted with many of the various approaches available.

Its simplicity is one of the best things about choices. A broad range of approaches are available, and all of them have a specific risk/reward profile. Certain approaches remain high-risk, such as risky call buying and put options; some are structured to prosper if reasonable assumptions of the future are fulfilled. People who really are inexperienced with options usually see them as a significant risk, based on speculation investment opportunities, and dismiss more progressive advantages offered by many trading strategies for (1) defending asset allocation roles, (2) propagating and hedging danger, and (3) creating extra profit on your shareholdings. Such 3 strategies make choices one of the most interesting and promising places to spend, and they are particularly effective when working with volatile commodity prices challenges.

They will concentrate on different option approaches available in the subsequent chapters that can be used to help defend your holdings and/or investments, mitigate risk, and increase your potential returns.

1.5 Take advantage of Options in Certain Circumstances

One of the main benefits of the choices is their versatility. You can earn a profit while you buy the stock if a thing is happening: the price of the product is going beyond the existing selling value. And yet options are still so adaptable that even if an inventory stays inside a limited price action, you can make again. Schedule spread and short traverses are two of the tactics intended to reap gains when the market price changes. This ensures that an options opportunity will be lucrative even though the stock displays relatively little action over the time of the open market.

Many tactics, such as lengthy straddles, are built to generate gains if the market price falls in any direction. In this scenario, what path the share price tries to move, and it moves, really doesn't matter. Since options could be utilized in many pairings, their programs are highly profound and rich. You would be well on the path to building successful tactics that function directly for you until you learn how to utilize time as the main factor in establishing benefit choice.

1.6 Using Options for Insurance

You can also use the options to "insure" your role. F or instance, if you purchase 1 place option for each and every 100 stock shares you own, this provides you security against the downside. The put can go up in value because the stock falls. And it doesn't matter how low the market price falls, and you are allowed to offer your shares at the putting option's strike price.

You may even guarantee a spot-on short order. If you've sold short stock, the worse outcome will be an upward market price. Through purchasing one call choice per every hundred shares, you sell short you will protect against that. The message goes rise in price as the market price increases. ' And again, you get the opportunity to purchase the stocks at the market price stated by call option, and it doesn't matter how high the market price is that.

You will use the options to protect the whole portfolio. On many various financial stocks, options are available such as Dow Jones, the S&p, and also the NASDAQ 75. Purchasing brings on the index closest to your investment composition provides protection against market danger. Whenever the equity demand declines, much of the securities in the fund are more expected to decline in price as well. However, the market puts are gaining in value, recouping most, if not any, of the stock's decline in value.

The Adventure Begins

The US financial markets contain one of the world's highest amounts of capital. So, someone with a limited sum of money will theoretically make income from it. What's it taking to succeed? Highest level investors and traders both agree that the secret to success is restraint, as, without it, you'll let a losing deal become an equity killer.

Awareness and preparation are important tools for effective options trading, but if you don't have the patience to execute a trading strategy, your attempts would certainly be in vain. To others, trade offers years of daunting struggles and a future of financial bonuses. Thankfully, this textbook will enable you to join this second category while you continue to understand options and integrate them through your current investing plan.

1.7 A Trader's Positive Attitude or winning mindset

To be a trader involves not only formulating improved tactics and carrying out more comprehensive analyzes but also having a positive attitude. In opinion to some traders' reports, what distinguishes a successful trader from just a failing one:

- o Successful traders will NOT devise superior trading tactics
- o Successful traders are NOT wiser
- o Successful traders will better business research.

Many traders falsely think that when they at first start trading, what they're doing is making a perfect strategy for trading. Afterward, all they'll have to do is arrive in the market every day, connect in their good trading plan, as well as the market just starts pumping cash into the account immediately.

Sadly, it is not much easy as some of us that have ever swapped have taught. There are loads of traders that use clever, well-built trading techniques and programs which often frequently lose a lot of money instead of making money.

The very some traders who regularly win the trading game are those that have established the effective behavioral attitude that makes it possible for them to win consistently. There are other values, behaviors, and personality variables that are important to the conquest of the trading region.

Identifying how trading operates

Successful traders recognize the variance between an "evil deal" and a money-losing transaction. It is a concept that is important to recognize. Even if you wind up spending money in a deal, it doesn't mean that it was a poor transaction – that also means it was a deal that was wasted. What renders a trade successful is not that it succeeds or fails – a trade is good as long if it provides more future gain than risk, so the chances or probability of performance are in the favor, irrespective of whether it works out to be. When, for fair purposes, you accept trade and handle the trade properly once you're in it, it's a good deal, even though you wind up being stopped for lost. (In comparison, even though a trade makes profits, if it was not conducted for good intentions and with a desirable risk/reward combination, then it is a poor deal, even if it may have turned out profitable).

Successful traders work on the assumption that if they carry on doing "healthy trades," as mentioned above, they would eventually be overwhelmingly profitable.

Losing traders misinterpret every trade that losses revenue as a "poor trade," as well as any trade that earns profits as a "healthy trade," irrespective of if there is a fair cause for doing the exchange – so this contributes to terrible, long-term trade loss. Evaluating transactions on the grounds only of either they manage to win or lose does nothing greater than aim for unpredictable bonuses equivalent to running a slot instrument.

Attitude towards the Market and You

Business values and behaviors cover issues like believing the economy is being skewed toward you. These detrimental – and incorrect – views will significantly affect the capacity to effectively exchange. When you look at the competition as out there to catch you, so you don't look at things correctly, in compliance with fact, and then you can't expect to be able to assess business possibilities critically. The economy is completely indifferent-whether you gain money or make a loss doesn't matter.

The beliefs concerning ourselves are vital aspects of psychological trade. One unique trait that nearly all successful traders express is body-confidence. Successful traders have a strong, intrinsic faith over their actions to be successful traders – a conviction not significantly shaken by a handful, or perhaps more, failing trades.

Most losing merchants, on the other side, have extreme, pestering self-doubt. Sadly, once you consider oneself as a loser dealer, afflicted by poor luck or something, then the conviction appears to become a promise the fulfills itself.

Traders who question their abilities frequently fail to press the button and start transactions, and thus, therefore, lose the chance for successful trading. We often prefer to cut short earnings, becoming unnecessarily pessimistic that the economy could at any moment transform against them. Successful traders get healthy regard for the reality that often, sometimes their strongest business forecasts may not suit potential demand fluctuations. Nevertheless, they have overwhelming trust in their abilities as traders – a faith that helps them to launch trades quickly if there is a real opportunity.

Main Characteristics of a Successful Trader

Emotionally, the quite best traders have the same main traits, including:

• They all feel confident taking risks. Those with very poor risk appetite, who cannot tolerate bad trades, really aren't cut out to be successful traders because bad trades are only part of the trading process. Successful traders should emotionally embrace the inevitable ambiguity of trade. Trading isn't like spending the capital with a fixed return on a bank plan.

• They're willing to adjust easily to rising business dynamics. They do not fall back in love with their analyzes of a business, just "marry." If market behavior suggests they need to adjust their opinions on possible future price changes, they do this without pause.

• They are diligent in their transactions and will approach the business critically, regardless of whether their cash balance is influenced by actual market activity

• They don't give way to getting too enthusiastic about successful trades or over-desperate for failing trades. Successful traders regulate their feelings rather than encouraging them to influence their feelings.

- They make the required efforts and take the appropriate measures to become self-disciplined dealers, working under specific principles of finance and risk assessment. Traders who win are not irresponsible gamblers. Until entering into any transaction, they carefully measure potential danger against the potential gain.

One of the successful traders' most significant psychological qualities is the willingness to recognize (1) ambiguity and (2) the possibility that you might well be incorrect more times than you are correct to launch trades. Successful traders recognize that conducting exchange is generally more of a talent than evaluating a business. Also, what defines gains and expenses is not so much a query about whether or when you reach a transaction, but much more a function of how you handle a transaction while you are in it.

Trading is a risk-filled activity.

Successful traders who truly embrace the challenge of trade have the potential to unhesitatingly reach a trading position and end a deal almost as quickly when it doesn't. They aren't saddled with the mental distress that results in losing concentration and self-confidence both as a consequence of an unworked exchange.

Traders that have not developed this approach towards trading are motivated by emotional responses to actually winning, or a bad trade and have not really embraced the reality that trade is a danger-filled company. If they do not behave in tune with reality, policymakers may not make the right trading choices possible.

Trading – and also being good at it – imposes immense pressure on us, perhaps even the expectation that we retain trust when grappling with the constant volatility of stock trading.

Telling the facts of what we're involved in in in the trading sector is one of the main factors for progress.

A good trader's upside-down emotional behavior

One cause why losing traders is so frequent is that certain habits and values that suit well in society do not fit well in the trading field at all. Many traders are oblivious of this reality and lack a clear idea of what trading actually is everything about.

We're told to prevent dangerous circumstances in our regular, everyday lives. Yet trading is mostly about risk-taking.

Attitudes to Win a Trade

Good traders study the trading success periodically and measure it. They realize that, over time, trading is indeed an art that is learned only by intensive practice.

Traders who compete are mobile. They are not ego-investing in their companies. They will interpret the competition critically and comfortably remove trade proposals that don't function at all.

Leading investors aren't hesitating to gamble capital whenever they see a possible profit incentive focused on business research and trading ideas. They aren't spending capital recklessly, though. Often mindful of the probability of becoming mistaken, they exercise stringent risk control by restricting their risks to limited amounts.

Comprehending that the market isn't predictable

Good traders are conscious and embrace the idea that the economy is inherently volatile, and there is no methodology or method for an examination of the business that can infallibly forecast price changes. Although they actually are keenly conscious of this reality, they look closely for indications whether their interpretation is incorrect, and when they see these signals, they change the trading stance quickly.

By comparison, failing traders, after they've placed on a deal, appear just to search for market volatility that indicates they're correct and eliminate or streamline some market behavior that appears to refute their research. And, sometimes, they wind up losing too long transactions and take disproportionately high losses.

Discipline and Freedom of a Trader

Trading is, in fact, boundless; the marketplace is a fully open place. At every moment in time, you are able to purchase or sell, join, or leave.

There are virtually no laws allowing you to open and close a deal at any specified price or period.

Given the fact one of the key benefits about trading is an utter ability to live our lives – essentially to do what we want anytime we like – the first and only way to be reliably effective in trading would be to soul-impose a collection in laws regulating our trade and to exercise rigid discipline in adhering to those laws.

What is the major issue? The question is, we all naturally enjoy the right to do anything we want and dislike getting certain laws and constraints imposed on us, including those of their own making.

Self-discipline is important for trade to be won.

Self-training is sadly usually the toughest training to get by. Almost everyone does a great job of adhering to the laws that are put on us beyond themselves, – for example a "no parking" notice, then to follow the laws that we make for oneself. Our mentality seems like one more like "Good, I've created the law, so I'm free to violate it." Although that's logically valid, it's not a mentality that's going to support you well during business.

A description of becoming a good trader

Trading is a challenging game to learn. Very little people are becoming extremely good at it. Practically everyone may, therefore, become a professional trader as far as they are able to make the requisite effort.

It requires thorough personality-analysis and personality-discipline to develop the correct emotional mentality for a successful trade. You have to know how to develop healthy trade practices since they are not items that come to most citizens automatically. Making the requisite improvements in oneself, which will help you to be a reliably successful trader, would more than probably affect how good you are coping with the current lifestyle but not how well you are coping with trade.

Simple truth: Invest in being a successful trader, and this will encourage you to be a successful trader. You may do it, so it's up to you to bring money for your account, not the economy.

The solution is inside of you.

Bad traders wrongly admit the secret to success is to conquer the competition itself. They refuse to address the fact of not being able to dominate the business. The competition is not controllable.

What you should monitor is yourself or what you're doing with the behavior of the company. Successful traders understand this reality and do more to control oneself and trading behavior than they do to control market research. It's not liked an overview of the business is not helpful. It's that the volume of knowledge accessible that can be regarded, and the quantity of specific technological or essential metrics, is almost infinite. Plus, what's important at one moment in time at some other moment in time can be completely meaningless.

It is just too many details to figure out and finally difficult to treat properly. The time a dealer focuses more on improving oneself and trading abilities.

Chapter 2: Spread trading

In finance, a spread may have many significances. Even so, they all simply apply to the disparity between the two values, levels, or returns. The most common meanings, the margin is the gap, like the stock, bond, or product, between the offer and the ask rates of a commodity or property. This is recognized as spreading bid-ask.

Spread may also apply to the disparity in a trading stance – the distance in between shorter stance with one futures market or dollar as well as a long position in the other. This is called officially as a commercial spread.

In financing, the premium may imply the change in the value charged to a protection issuer and the cost paid by the buyer for such security — that is, the expense to purchase a problem that an insurance broker charges relative to price the insurer offers it to the market.

That spread in lending may also apply to the amount a borrower spends to have a loan over a benchmark rate. For e.g., if the main interest level is 3%, and a consumer pays a mortgage fee of 5%, the gap is 2%.

2.1 Spread Trading Overview

Most private market participants are forward traders. Generally speaking, that involves owning a share or corporate bond with both the hope that the share or common fund 's value will increase with time. Linear trade is dangerous since the equilibrium of factors at some moment on time that decides the worth of an asset is most probably to move this in one path or something other. You already hold the inventory for $9 if you purchase an inventory at $10, so it losses 10 percent of its interest. In order to no loss or no gain point, the inventory now must boost through $1 and 11 percent.

What about if $2 dropped the inventory, you lost 20 percent of one's capital expenditure. Until you reach break-even, the stock will grow around $8 or $10 or 25 percent. /So, if you missed $5 / 50% of your savings, the inventory would still have to increase to $5 - $10 until break-even, because you must have a 100% return!

This book teaches you when to use spread investing to win.

Spread commerce is the procedure of buying one choice deal and selling a connected option simultaneously, for example, two options with the relevant class (calls/puts) but specifically implied vol and/or expiry dates.

Spread betting is utilized by options investors and derivatives investors to lower the chance of missing significant amounts from a rapid price change.

Spread investing will produce 20 percent to 30 percent annualized earnings with limited risk or even without danger. Total returns of more than 100 percent or more are achievable through growing the risk appetite while also expose yourself to a slightly lower risk than experienced by positional trading. And why is it that not everybody spreads trade? So why not allow the use of options? There's a common assumption that choices are dangerous. First of all, it must be remembered that incentives have been implemented as a way to mitigate risk efficiently. The right implementation of options in the context of different strategies, including spread trading, allows trading of individuals with lower risk in a structured manner. Given an investor knows trading tools options, there is little need to make options dangerous as the costs and benefits of any particular transaction are understood at all periods.

To sum up, knowledge about options trading tools reduces the risk of trading options.

And in a quick illustration, let's equate the dangers involved with selling options and trading platforms.

Spread betting is really the process of buying another option product and selling a similar one concurrently, for example, two options with the same type (calls/puts) with separate strike rates or expiry dates.

Stock Example:

So, let's presume ABC stock sells at $10 a share, and I'd like to purchase 100 stock shares. The price I'll have pay is the basis for my rate.

Inventory Cost Base = 100 times $10 = $1000 Options illustration: options are usually acquired in transactions where there are 100 stocks of inventory in a deal.

Now, if I had to purchase one option deal composed of 100 shareholdings at a market price of $10, typically, a purchase amount could be $1.50 for every share.

Option Price Base = 100 shares times $1.50/share = $150 So I need to expend $1000 to regulate 100 shareholdings of the stock across a stock offering, whereas I can regulate the same amount of stock with such an alternative for just a portion of the capital, just $150. So, I have to lose $1000 with stocks; however, with options, can gamble just a fraction of the capital yet still retain the same leverage.

Buying stock has been considered a horizontal trade because only if the price goes off one path – up, you earn money in your investment! As you can see in the following sections, distributing investing helps you to earn profits as the price swings in either direction, whether upwards, downwards, or even static.

The terms of the solutions will be clarified later. The complexities at this stage should not be grasped, only the general definition.

2.2 Directional Trading Vs. Spread Trading

Directional Trade Benefits:

• Higher benefit opportunity

• Greater risk potential

• Quick-term changes acquire Sufficient momentum to take advantage.

Drawbacks

• Increased danger because income is just one momentum

• Needs greater capital spending

• Market volatility would have a larger effect on spending.

2.3 Greed and Fear

Demand and supply can impact market price shifts. When equity values increase, greed may control investors in a market's place, and, as rates decline, terror will rule sellers' mentality.

The willingness to transact critically by suppressing all greed and terror is a vital key to prosperity, and the strategy for doing this might be illustrated later. At this point, it is necessary to remember that it's one of their prime goals.

2.4 Swing trading

Swing trade is a simple form of short-time market manipulation in which shares are kept for more than one day. It may be used for forex, stocks, futures, options, cryptocurrency, and ETFs trading. This page will provide a deep look at the nature of swing investing, with several tactics and advice for top strategies. It will also examine the dangers and benefits of swing trading, together with daily charts and indicators, before finishing up with certain key take-off points.

What is Swing Trading?

The basic concept for newcomers of swing investing is where people seek to catch profits by keeping an asset anytime from immediately to multiple weeks. As the training guides stress, the aim is to leverage a greater market change than is achievable in such an intraday timeframe. But since you're pursuing a wider price spectrum and change, you'll need measured role sizing to minimize downside risk.

For this purpose, people call for technical analyzes to identify quick-term price progress instruments. This means respecting the principles and fundamentals of price movements and trends.

Setups and methodologies of swing trading are primarily conducted by people rather than large institutions. That's because large companies generally trade in dimensions that are too big to swiftly exit and enter securities. Even so, as examples would prove, retail investors will profit on market swings in the short term.

Swing Trading Benefits

As blogs and forums can illustrate easily, swing trading has many benefits, including

• Implementation – Swing trade may be used across a broad range of stocks and tools. You should focus on the new altcoins, for example, including a bitcoin, Ethereum (ETH), and Litecoin. Alternatively, regular options encourage you to continue to swing trading.

• Tools – Online services exist to support you be one of the great successes. eBooks, online training programs, PDFs, applications, instructional classes, and a whole range of websites are available. All will have suggestions for forex tactics, general trading plans, and top pattern-identification tips. Additionally, enter the chat Discord to engage in an effective trading strategies party.

• Software – You can move trading on any variety of sites, from Bit stamp to Meta-trader, to use candlesticks as well as other techniques. There is the option of using computerized bots or expert consultant software. Used properly, this will allow you to do much more position power than you could ever manually do.

• Mentality – As personal stories indicate, if you have the characteristics essential for day-to-day trading efficiently, you will well have the ones needed to swing trading. Is you patient, for example? Do you mind injuries from major stops? Are you able to perform fewer trades while remaining careful about the few installations that you're doing? If indeed, the characteristics and skill of a good swing trader can already be yours.

Risks

There are other pitfalls, including:

• Market danger – Rule 101 – they will certainly lose money until you hang up your career to start swing-trading for a profit. Though others have makes it look simply, your income can feel any errors where it affects the most. And indeed, as is the essence of business trading, lessons are still taught in a hard way. Additionally, margin trading and using power and influence might see you losing much more your original cost.

• Duration – Swing trading wasn't one of the forms of trading that you can join and test your place a week or two away. It is a live trade that needs clear monitoring and the techniques that function. That may be difficult to juggle swing trade with such a full-time job.

• Taxation – Swing exchange will not automatically exclude you. In reality, you could get swept up in trend day trader laws in the US, for instance. So, verify that first, you will meet some commitments of your financial structure.

• Managing risk – If you're investing in a stock market or use an algorithm program, failure to execute an appropriate risk management plan and financial planning might cost you a lot. As profitable broker Harry Lite retorted, "I have constantly been witnessing instances of many other people across my financial life that I have regarded being destroyed by a lack of respect for risk. If you don't take a good look at danger, this will take you.

• Psychology-Do you want a fast-moving, competitive market environment? Have you frustrated with a desire to know instantly if you are right or wrong? If so, you do not have the attitude required to be a billionaire and swing-trading master.

Those are by no ways the swing trading rules package. You may also use the above on the checklist to watch whether your millions of dreams already seem tight.

Day Trading vs. Swing Trading

The biggest distinction is the time a place retains. Day trade, as the name implies, involves closing shares until the business day is done. Furthermore, as chart trends indicate when they swing trade, they carry on the possibility of overnight discrepancies against your place rising up or down. As a consequence, you frequently take a lower place size while swinging trading than you would be a day trading because intraday investors also use power to take greater sizes of place.

That said, swing traders will gain on a nighttime margin of up to 50 percent. But as courses and guidance from recently retired traders will figure out, swinging margin trading can be severely risky, especially when there are margin calls.

So, flipping trade or day trade isn't really about what you need to deal in, be it resources or oil futures or CAL 40 stocks.

Instead, it's just the time. Thus, although the day trader looks at four hourly and regular charts, the shift trader would be more involved with inter-day charts and movements of candlesticks. In reality, some of the more common include:

- Triangles
- Cup-and-handle trends
- Double bottoms
- Moving average convergence
- Heads and shoulders formations
- Shooting stars

Flags One final day's distinction in swing trade vs. scalping between day trading with the option of stop-loss techniques. Stop-losses are usually larger for swing trading to match the reasonable benefit goal.

What Stocks to Swing Trade

Among the first lessons you'll know from instructional tutorials, videos, or user manuals is because you need the best investments to pick from. For starters, in forms of inventory, large-cap inventories always have the quantity and liquidity ratios you need. Typically, these shares move among higher elevations and extreme lows. That means they can move in one path for a couple of days and instead switch to the other side of both the exchange when you see reversal trends.

Some of the fundamentals of swing planning is picking accurate investment choices. Choosing a site with powerful screeners or scanners is a helpful tip to get you to the goal. If you are theorizing on the incorrect low-priced products, there is absolutely no point in getting the correct approach.

The Right Market

In both extremes of the market, a bear market atmosphere, or the raging bull sector, swing trading could be especially challenging. There you can note that only extremely productive inventories will not show the very same up-and-down fluctuations because when indices were steady for weeks at the top.

Instead, you'll note the momentum in a bull or bear market would usually push stocks in one direction for a considerable time. This will indicate the optimal point of entry and approach is focused on the pattern in the longer term.

Essentially instead, you have the perfect swing-trading climate because the shares are not going somewhere. For e.g., if you wanted to sell on the Nasdaq, you'd like the index to grow for a few days, fall for a few days, and instead reverse the trend. So even if your stock could be all over initial levels after several months, you have had various chances to capitalize on short-time fluctuations.

Using the Exponential Moving Average

A swing trading college can bring warnings, holes, focal points, and critical indicators for you. But maybe the (EMA) is one of the key concepts that they can talk you around.

This is essentially a variant of the standard moving average, but the emphasis on the recent data points is enhanced. Used properly, this can help you determine trend transmissions as well as points of entry and exit much quicker than an easy moving average could. Basically, the EMA plotline can be used to construct your entry/exit strategy.

Application

An EMA program is simple and can display techniques for learners of a swing trade. The 9-, 13- or 50-period EMA may be used. Upon starting beneath, the bullish convergence will occur at the stage when the stock crosses over the trend lines.

This informs you of a turnaround, and maybe an uptrend is about to fall into action. If then your EMA nine-period exceeds the EMA 13-period, this will alert you to a lengthy entry. This being mentioned, a 13-period moving average must be over, or simply cross over, a 50-period EMA.

On the positive side, if the cost for a resource falls underneath the EMAs, a bearish spinoff happens. This shows you there might be a possible pattern turnaround. You will instead see this from a long place to the time of your departure.

And if the EMA's nine-period crosses the EMA's 13-period, this will alert you to a quick entrance or the want to leave a long spot. Have also said, the take at least 13 period EMA needs to be below or cross just below 50-period EMA.

Using the EMA properly, with the correct time periods and protection in your sights, and you'll have all the basics of a successful swing technique.

Psychology of Swing Trading

It's real that you will access a whole range of audiobooks, podcasts, and PDFs, which will show you explanations of swing investing, laws to obey, and maps to create for Heiken-Ashi. What they don't really tell you though, is how to respond emotionally when the swing trading plan doesn't succeed.

All that explained, you have three ideas to consider:

1. Get a schedule and adhere to it – Rises and drops will be there, that's the very essence of purchase and sale in the stocks. Let the numbers decide the ups and downs; however, don't let your feelings get towards the way. Choosing when and how to sell will easily transform into an emotional choice when you get your entire weeks back on the table. You devise a plan, and then faithfully adhere to it.

2. Fighting uncertainty by raising risk – The desire for danger is special for all. So, find the right risk criteria. You would

want to continue with not losing more than 2 percent of your margin requirement in a single transaction, for example. No coach will explain that to you. You can only know where the own boundaries are by weeks of practice.

3. Plan for wide-term – So many traders is concerned with last or next exchange. Don't panic if it's all gold futures that you lose. Instead, the worry of the amount and calculation for long-term benefit. Like jeff Kovner appropriately points out, "You can't compete if you individualize defeats."

Swing Trading Top Tips

Also, many of the better forex guides left out some swing trading's favorite tricks and secrets, including

• Using the press – Stocks are continually changing in response to press happenings. Other outlets, such as Google Finance or CNBC, can use the number, price activity, and weekly graphs to include market insight and analysis. The news may, therefore, help you identify possible opportunities and income securities, for instance, to keep a close eye on. It might encourage you to prepare your entrances and exits, too.

• Never stop yourself from seeking knowledge – As Chris Tudor Anderson recently said: "The trick to being efficient from a business viewpoint is to get a tireless and everlasting and insatiable appetite for understanding and expertise." A lot of knowledge is ready to help you create successful crypto or forex techniques. For e.g., video guides will help you teach Gann strategies as well as how to begin using the money choices weekly in detail. We can even take you via indications about your MT4 framework and regular stock updates setting up.

• Choose the correct exchange & broker – all have specific requirements and goals, and whilst a crypto trader may be better placed on Gdax and Binance, an extremely successful foreign exchange swing trader might want to try Dailyfx. Do remember they are more than a location to find quotations and stock trading. They may help you create a watch list, portfolio, and more.

- Maintain a Diary – It will prove useful to hold an Excel file. Just write down the location, time, size of the place, and a purpose for exit and entry points. This might help us see why, for instance, the currency pair breakouts strategy doesn't fit on weekly maps.

How Much Money Can You Make?

The returns on swing trading entirely depend mostly on the dealer. Take utilized ETFs versus stocks, for example, some can deliver lucrative returns with both the greater while miserably disappointing with the first, given the fact that both trades are relatively close.

It'll also rely partly on the path you choose. Some users are going to support MACD metrics when some are using NMA. Much like others would swear while utilizing candlestick forecasting with rates of encouragement and opposition, whilst others would exchange on the press.

The trick is to find a solution that fits your timetable for you.

Final Thoughts

While distinct from day trading, feedback and tests say swing trading could be a neat method to continue with for beginners. It is intraday trading that will prove very hectic in hundreds of securities. Although swing traders can see their gains within a few days, retaining strong incentive rates. Around the same moment, shift trading is quick enough to avoid disruption over lengthy-term trading.

What's more, the specifications are small. You need an investment account or some cash, but by then, you'll find all the online gurus support you need to try to reap money. In addition, trading options could be effective in a vast range of retailers.

Yet while it might be fairly easy to know how to begin swing trading like either a part-time and full-time work, the money is at danger. Caution, however, must be given at every time.

Chapter 3: Using call option for income and speculation

It's best to grasp the terms and guidelines of options before you begin trading it. You have to build a comprehensive knowledge of danger farther than that, and how much it differs from one approach to the next. Note that alternatives may be found in a broad range of ways, varying from cautious to quite dangerous. Often investors are first drawn to high-leverage tactical trading options. Linear trading is where an investor feels he understands how a stock price swings and creates a chance to take favor of it.

With inventory, you have just one thing to care about — price. You have 3 changing metrics in the options landscape: the overall market price, the average fall in time, and uncertainty. The valuation of the options would be influenced by adjustments in any of these. We have discussed before how adjustments in the margin requirement price affect the value of the puts and calls. Time is also another term that can be taken relatively quickly. In any option approach, the reality that options can expire and can become useless in the long term is an essential and important feature; eventually, it can decide whether the option trading choices are efficient or not.

The impact volatility used on a valuation of the options is typically easier to grasp for beginners. Preferably, all the markets want to learn is what potential uncertainty would feel like. But as we don't realize either, we are trying to infer what it's going to be. The place to start for this supposition is mathematical (often referred to as cultural) uncertainty, or SV. The SV informs us what the real variance was during a given time period for the stock. Even then, there is also another volatility factor called implicit risk, or IV, which is used by traders to determine if the options are cheap or costly.

There are many various pricing strategies types available, but most should deliver a quality that is fairly similar to one another. When you add in all the factors (stock price, interest rate, time, dividends and liquidity), you get an answer that informs you what an option would be worth, depending on those figures. And what if you work backwards on the model? You know, after all, what the alternative is to trad. You will also figure out with a bit of analysis the other factors (interest rates, stock price, dividends, and the period remaining in the option). In reality, the first and only aspect you don't know at this point is what will become potential volatility.

You get the trading price when you add all those figures in and function the pricing model reverse, so-called since it is the variance indicated by the actual price of the contract. So, IV is determined on the basis of the choice incentives already exchanged. Option investors sometimes claim "Strong Premium Rates" or "Small Premium Rates." Whatever they actually imply is higher or lower current IV. If you grasp this idea, so it makes perfect sense that while their rates are low, you will want to purchase options, and selling options while they are costly.

Your trade options strategy will always be focused mostly on the amount of danger you believe is acceptable. Many investors allow the use of options as an area of a wider asset picking approach. Therefore, the appropriate beginning point is an analysis of the basic and technological measures. Next, we describe some simple techniques for trading options using calls. We should discuss the usage of calls to comment on the stock course with

Just a quick buy and scatter debit order. Then we'll look at how calls can be used to produce incremental profits by protected call writes or credit spreads. We're going to think a bit about LEAPS 'particular situation, and how it could be used as a stock replacement. Our purpose here is to illustrate how you can maximize your investment returns without leading yourself to unacceptable threats.

3.1 The Long Call Strategy—Using Calls for Speculation

Many investors continue by purchasing stock, and are accustomed to thinking about buying a stock because of its ability to grow in price. But typically, new option buyers start purchasing call options merely because it's close to some of what they are therefore used and do. If a call option is bought on stock (also called "going long the contract"), the call buyer will be able to manage that stock before actually owning it, and can do so at a percentage of the rate. Buying calls is one of the most common tactics among investors since the initial launch of listed options. A trader will have a clear knowledge of purchasing and keeping put options before going on to more complex strategies.

The long call is an option leveraged against the product itself. If the market price decreases, the value of the option rises by a percentage or more (sometimes even more). This leverage will result in high percentage gains, as buying calls needs a smaller initial capital investment than purchasing the stock straight away. Your earnings are in effect technically infinite, because there is no cap on how far a stock price will go. Even this approach has reduced risk, as you can't lose as much as you charged for the right. Although the possible loss in dollars is minimal, however, you will lose 100 per cent of the premium charged for a call. The output graph on the territory sheet shows the (restricted) danger for a long call approach and the infinite possible benefit.

The three straight lines in the preceding figure show graphically how volatility affects the place. The red line reflects the potential output of the long call as of now, the strong line reflects the output at expiry (the next trade day), as well as the yellow dot reflects the success of this choice halfway between now and expiry. Note also that convergence of every line with a $0 benefit line reflects the break-even stage in the time frame, and as time progresses, that break-even position travels further to the side.

The problem is now: What choice would I buy? The growing stock which trades stocks has a minimum four separate months of expiry with.

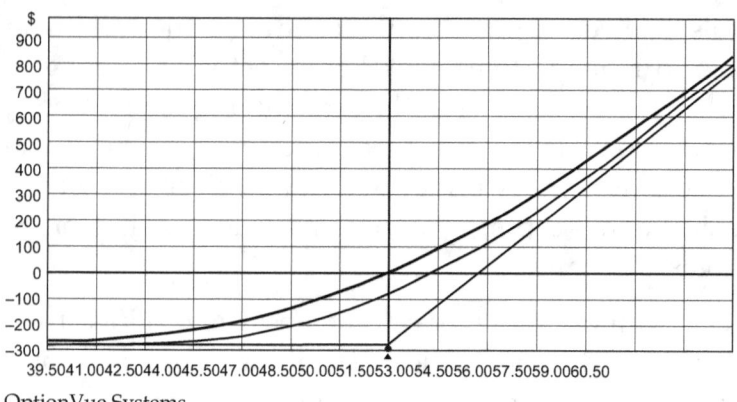
OptionVue Systems

Lots of different prices available for a strike. Based on the option time and cost left before maturity, options react in many various ways to price fluctuations in the portfolio.

Out: of-the-money stocks are named calls with selling values greater than the existing trading price; if the termination date was today, they would be useless. Out of the-money calls still retain interest if the market price already requires room to climb past the strike level. The portion of the period due price of an opportunity is referred to as time interest or time prime.

An at-the-money option is those whose selling price is the equal (or rather similar in practice) of the purchase price.

The price charged for an at-the-money alternative is attributed solely to time again. Of course, having this an in-the-money decision isn't going to require much of a rise in market price.

The on-the-money call choice is offered at a value greater than the existing market price. The distinction, called its fundamental value, between the market price and the existing stock price is the amount that the option will be in the funds. But then as far while there is time left before the termination day, there would still be some time advantage of an in-the-money alternative, which ensures that an option's price may be divided into two parts: the inherent value and the opportunity cost. After that, there is a diagram illustrating how the price of such an option is divided into inherent interest and time cost, based on whether it's at, near, or out of the market.

Stock Price at $50

Call Strike	Option Price ($)	Time Value ($)	Intrinsic Value ($)	ATM, OTM, or ITM
60.00	0.50	0.50	0.00	Out-of-the-money
55.00	2.00	2.00	0.00	Out-of-the-money
50.00	4.00	4.00	0.00	At-the-money
45.00	7.00	2.00	5.00	In-the-money
40.00	10.50	0.50	10.00	In-the-money

The more an alternative is out of the budget, the easier it would be, and the greater the leverage. And, if the inventory makes a fast push in your direction, the best job of maximizing your money will be an out-of-the-money choice. But, if this step doesn't happen fast, the efficiency of the out-of-the-money alternative would undoubtedly mislead everyone. At-the-money or in-the-money calls are moved much like the company's securities, as their delta is larger. Usually, the variance for the at-the-money choice is around .50 — meaning a one-point change in supply converts into a half-point shift for the contract. In-the-money contracts have deltas reaching one and transfer with demand virtually point-for-point. The optimal combination of considerations will also be sought utilizing options at-the-money, or merely in-the-money.

There are many opportunities to purchase shares. Many that want to engage in market price appreciation but lack the money to buy it directly will obtain an alternative for a quarter of the price. The restricted risk relates to certain investors who want to restrict their risks to just the option's quality. Eventually, there are many individuals that swap options to take full advantage of the necessary power while speculating on market changes.

3.2 The Bull Call Spread — An Alternative to the Long Call Strategy

We also reported that early option traders appear to begin buying calls. No, they would find the value of the spread. The spread of bull calling is used when you expect that a given stock's price should rise but needless chance than you can get with such a call purchase. It means purchasing a call option at the same rate, thus offering another put option at the greater market price within the same month of expiry. The greatest downside of a bull sell spread is whether it diminishes the consequences of longer options — time and uncertainty of the two main rivals. This is less prone to everyday market price volatility because it's a more casual form of trading. Another advantage of extending a short call over the put option is that you are investing less money on an equivalent number of contracts. This lowers the break-even level and creates the chance of profit-taking.

You purchase options from 1 strike price in a long call spread and sell someone at a higher price — the calls they are offering lower the purchasing price of a call you are receiving. Let's claim, for example, a stock that currently trades at $90 provides calls at 100 and 110 hits. A Hundred calls cost $6, as well as the $110s worth $4. So, it will charge you $600 to purchase one of 100 calls. But with the spread of the bull call, you might purchase the 100 strikes at $600, and offer the 110s at $400, which would save you the $200 net difference. But you might manage to purchase several of a Bull option spreads for the cost of an individual call contract. Then what's the bear call sharing maximum danger and benefit ability?

Bad case: when the market price will not increase beyond $100 until expiry, the entire deal (plus selling costs) would cost you $200 each spread.

Better case: You'll prosper if the market price reaches or tops $110 a share by the expiry date. Your benefit would be the disparity between both the hits ($10) subtract the expense of spreading ($2) for the 100 stocks, with a gross gain of $800 on each split you have ordered.

The figure in this topic below, shows the entire spectrum of opportunities for such a technique.

In the above case, at the market price for 100, you will have to pay $600 on each call, and all is the transaction cost. But the scatter of the bull's calls just cost everyone $200. Placing $600 in a-time-value call is a very dangerous tactic. Selling a call at a greater strike price covers most of the loss only with spread, so the chance is significantly smaller. Options are costlier in conditions of extreme uncertainty.

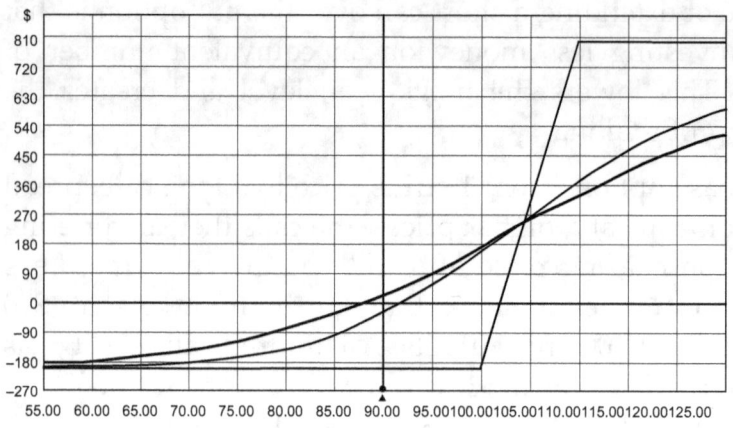

Which puts a buyer's choice at a loss? Nonetheless, through selling the overly expensive option at a very same time as he purchases an outrageously expensive option, the call or put spreader manages to subdue most of this impact.

3.3 The Covered Call – Generating Additional Income from Your Stock Portfolio

Protected reporting is also praised as a secure way to produce extra profits from a portfolio of stocks. It simply follows from the basic buying of products, is fairly simple to describe, and contributes to instant sales. But it seems as secure as spending merely in stock. Although risky call investors typically keep their place for a fairly short time period, the protected call author also plans to hang on until the expiry of their role. The greatest thing is that protected authors earn money because their portfolio portfolios get anywhere across times. With a total profit of 30 percent or more, the profits produced may be remarkable. Note, though; these gains are only likely if the market goes upward or continues at about the same level.

There have been two options to offer "exposed" or "protected" calls. This is a bare call where a sold contract has no insurance or other role that reduces or lowers the risk. Owning 100 stock options per each offered put option hedges a call option and reduces some of the harm. Additionally, the option may be a great call at a particular strike date, as mentioned earlier in the long call spread approach.

Do note that an offer is a deal, with various privileges and responsibilities for sellers and buyers. When you purchase a call option, it ensures you have the opportunity to acquire 100 stocks at the agreed strike price. The holder of the call option may enforce the right upon you when they sell calls. When the buyer choice wants to exercise its freedom, you, as a seller, are obligated to supply the required amount of securities at the agreed price (strike). The risk of the exposed call strategy seems to be that the price of the stock can increase above the call option strike price you've offered. In this scenario, you will need to sell 100 stocks at the agreed market price, which may be significantly lower than the stock's existing market value. For the presence of other people; thus, the possibility of writing undisclosed calls is unreasonable.

So, to escape the chance, you have to hedge a sell option. The plan is no more high-risk if you buy 100 stock options and offer a call upon the money. In the case of an activity, you control the 100 securities and will actually supply them to fulfill the statutory requirements of the request being exercised. A protected call writer wants income mainly. You do get certain insurance against the risk (by the sum of the bonus you earn). However, the balancing act is what offered call reduces the overall potential benefit. But as far as you wisely choose the strike price, this may be a fruitful tactic. Let's assume you actually purchased 100 stock shares at $36 a share, for instance. You offer a 40 request and get a $2 discount. If you need $200 to offer the order, the market base is reduced down towards $34 per share: Initial selling price

$3,600 Less: bid premium−200 Converted cost base $3,400 Under this case, you'll benefit in the event of an exercise, but the overall income is $6 per share (you need $4,000 it doesn't matter how big the market price at a moment of the exercise). If a share price fell to $34, you'd get a massive loss. The gamut of income and deficit is outlined in the following figure:

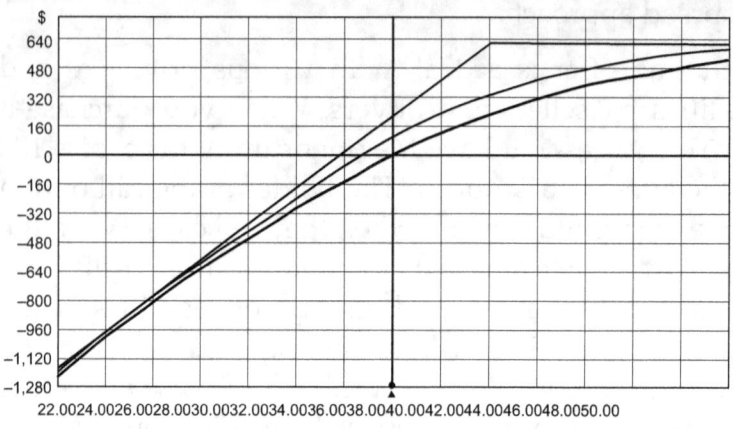

If the purchase price is more than $40 a stock by expiry, the value is in the "fair benefit zone," and you can gain $600 mostly on payment: purchase price − 100 shares − $4,000 Reduced purchase base − − 3,400 Fixed income at exercise $-600 The amount just below deep discount mark is the "loss limit." You risk $1 a share on any point a stock drop under $32 every stock, just like you're going to pay. Yet note, the stocks were actually bought at $34 a dollar.

For this instance, it is the center range that illustrates the benefit of selling protected calls. As far as stock holds around $34 to $40 a share, the call is best suited for you to sell. The short call may terminate worthlessly, so you may end it with a close order. If the call ends or is purchased to complete, the cycle will then be reversed by offering another request. You can replay the series as much if you want.

Covered call authors have a strong edge overexposed call authors since the workout isn't disastrous. It merely suggests that you have the premium offer, and also sell the 100 stock shares at a profit. You keep earning dividends as far as you get the property, too. The exposed call composes three potential outcomes:

1. You shut the position down. Use a close buy trade, and you will still cancel a short spot. Throughout this situation, you start with an initial auction; if the put option falls in value later, you can buy back and shut the spot. The disparity between the "sell" and "buy" rates is income, which is recorded this year. The place is closed as a quick-term dividend income.

2. The option drops out useless. There's always a risk a short in out-of-the-money request place will never get interested in the market. When maturity comes close, the margin requirement starts to vanish rapidly. It is useless at depletion. In this scenario, the whole compensation is income, which is stated that year the right expired as just a short-time capital gain.

3. You exercise the right. The third point is fitness. If the investor chose to exercise, it would call off the 100 shares at the purchase price, so you will have the premium received. This always occurs when the price of the inventory is greater than the price of the hit, thereby rendering it an opportunity in the capital. Exercise will actually occur at any moment, and you need to be ready for this likelihood if you offer an order.

As a general thumb rule, offering protected calls only makes sense if you are totally able to get your share capital called up. But, if the valuation of the stock is increasing and below the market price of the protected bid, you may want to stop exercise. You would achieve so by swapping one call with another for an auction named "rolling up." You might close the margin requirement with a buy contract, with the example, and then offer another calling opportunity at a higher market price in a longer month. You will roll up out, and forever as far as you will be able to buy selling the 100 stocks to protect the sell call place, the stock price begins to grow.

Although time decaying is a major issue for buyers of options, it's the secret to sellers of options achieving performance. The lower the value of the right decreases, the more money you produce. The true benefit of covered sales opportunities is not just that you may produce profits with no added expense, and that you could replicate the cycle again and again. You will offer another call over the same 100 stocks when each choice opportunity is shut or ends worthless — and replay it as many occasions as you want. So, the 100 shares will generate gains not only from stock growth and income, but from premium call.

But the protected call approach does have some drawbacks. First, if the inventory is going up fast, even doubling or tripling in size, the income is small. But of course, first, you purchased the stock anticipating it to grow in value. So, you were it! Sadly, you'll reap very small from it in this situation as the call offered restricts your profits.

Then if market price declined dramatically? Your calls offer so little actually to shield you from damages when the price sinks. You get to retain the bonus from selling your call, but you also have stock that needs way below than you charged for.

Not everybody can sell calls, especially those who anticipate a very rapid acceleration of the stock price. While being a competitive technique, it functions well as part of a larger investment plan. Understand just what potential consequences could happen and be able to track your roles carefully so that you can respond whenever you have to. It is a cautious approach for those that already appreciate the protected call that can greatly boost returns on investment.

3.4 Long-Term Speculation — The Special Case of LEAPS

LEAPS — Long Duration Equity Expectation Securities — are options that have a far greater period than normal shares, with a time span of years, not months. Just about 10 percent of available stocks include LEAPS, the most common high-volume stock mainly. LEAPS have a substantial time benefit and are much more costly than regular options but nevertheless less than buying 100 stock shares. You may think of them in several ways as an alternative to purchasing the product.

LEAPS were used mainly for inference. As suggested by their titles, if you expect a long-term stock price increase, you could purchase the call LEAPS, or a place LEAPS if you believe the stock value is expected to decline for a long period. Although the danger graph for a long LEAPS call location looks just like a long call seen earlier, any extra danger is introduced by the longer time frame. The high time premium correlated with LEAPS especially implies they are vulnerable to shifts in high vol. There's no worse feeling than to see the economy leap in the expected direction while earning precious little of your shares. Contemporary volatility maps are accessible from best-optioned platforms and tech firms like Option Vue Platforms Global, and such maps will help you decide whether stock options are traditionally cheap or costly.

LEAPS may also be used as a stock substitute in tactics such as the just described covered order. You will buy the long-term LEAPS options in that plan, and sell a short-term option at the same amount. The short choice is protected, or hedged, by the long alternative LEAPS. Technically, that's a horizontal array, or calendar, actually. Yet here you will add several of the same strategies from the protected call approach, like rolling the short opportunity when it is opened or expires worthlessly. And despite the time value differences, you may also profit from playing the spread timing clearly. Later in this guide, we should explore the horizontal distribution, and you will be comfortable with the related dangers before seeking it out. The argument, though, is that due to their low time value, LEAPS offers tremendous versatility.

3.5 The Bear Call Spread — Collecting Income from Option Selling

The distribution of the bull call is a constrained-risk approach that effectively benefits of the time interest decay. For one way, it's the very reverse of the distribution of the market call; you're looking for a stock-decline. You purchase a spread of a stock call, thinking it will raise its value, not as with a portfolio. But with the spread of the bull call, when you put the exchange, you earn a payment to your bank, and your intention is to retain it. The credit that you are getting is your future income. You will never render more. Even so, if a stock rises, you will lose it and more. And with a sell call spread, you will earn money if the market price does not change between then and maturity at all. You really don't want to see things moving up.

You sell a put option at such a lower market price to create a bear option spread and counter it by purchasing a put option at a better strike price much farther out of the bank. For e.g., let's assume you have 50 or 55 put options accessible on a $48 stock that you think would decline, with both the 50 calls priced at $5, as well as the 55 calls priced at $3. Also, because 50 calls are similar to the actual selling level, you'll get a net profit for this form of exchange.

If a stock decreases in valuation, the valuation of the 50 calls that you sell would also decrease. They can either be closed for the benefit or can expire worthlessly. The only justification for purchasing the strikes at a high call option calls would be to lower your risk in case you're incorrect, and the price goes up. That means the full exposure to the danger is proportional to the gap between the hits, excluding the premium earned when the spread of the market call opened.

From the above case, per each 50–55 split you created, you will get paid $200, minus service fees. Thus, the average sensitivity to danger would be $300. You might close the place and take another net loss if the stock was to ever grow. The worst possible outcome is when you were practicing the quick 50 calls until you could start shutting. You'd then be expected to offer $50 in 100 shares. With the distribution of bear calling, you can still practice your 55 requests to fulfill the criteria, losing a total of $300 on a transaction.

In this case, the bear sell spread will be attractive as far as a stock ends at or around $52 a share even by expiry date. In the spread of the bull call, your future assets and liabilities are minimal, so even in a second case, your benefit will only be greater than the original credit earned. The potential effects of this exchange are seen in the figure below.

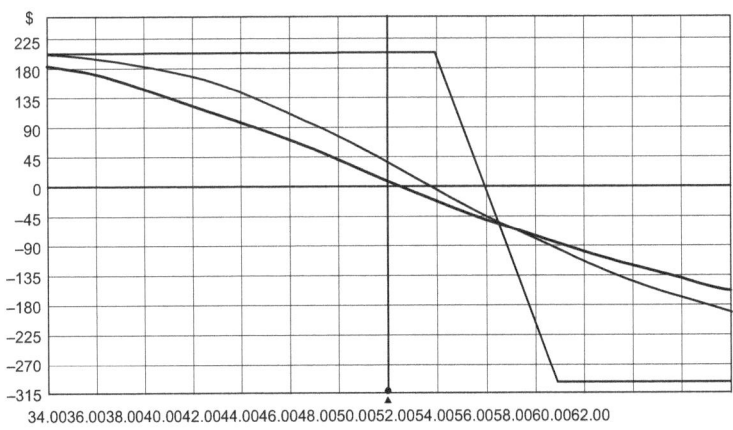

OptionVue Systems

Unlike the bull put spread, when you merely pay the variance in the two options' premiums, the credit spread requires a margin condition that is dependent on the disparity in the strike rates. You will have to bring up the loss between the rates of the strike (in this scenario 5, or $500 each spread) less the money you got (in this situation $200). This ensures that positioning the exchange would cost you just $300.

Note, any option approach that looks nice on paper can only succeed if the residual stock is acting in any way. You will devise plans that would be efficient if the stock shifts in a certain direction; unless the stock falls within a target range; or if movement happens inside the time limits set on all of the options. Yet even the derivatives dealer needs to be alert for the unpredictable. Price unpredictability characterizes markets, and it describes the danger of options to a greater extent.

3.6 A Word on Risk Management

You will recognize the possible risk and the possible advantage when joining a deal with both choice approaches, and be able to consider the risk if anything does happen. Stock investors who are effective year after year can testify that managing risk is the secret to long-term productivity, especially restricting the possible loss to a fixed percentage point of your brokerage account for each transaction. The most widely quoted statistic is 5 percent in discussions with many of these people, which indicates that no exchange will cost greater than 5 percent of the brokerage account. A percentage greater than that raises the likelihood that your decision will be clouded with emotion. Your trade operation might then bring on a more gambling-close aspect. Simple truth: Manage risk carefully by each trade's possible loss to 5 percent of the trading portfolio.

Chapter 4: Using puts for speculation, protection and income

Westerners are realists; we believe everything, including market markets, should look better future. So, we obviously prefer to support put options, since we'll make a good profit as the market price rises. Yes, as actively managed stocks were launched in 1973, there are no usable put options, just calls! Using equity options didn't start selling until 4 weeks later, in July 1977. However, the truth is that even the various financial markets (as well as the specific securities that they comprise) do not all go up, but do have lengthy bearish action seasons. Put options to purchase helps you to reap as it occurs.

We outlined a number of possible uses for long positions in the subsequent segment, with a focus on betting and profits. We describe throughout this chapter when to utilize two techniques — the short put as well as the bear placed spread — while speculating through an imminent price decline. We'll also see at economic generating possibilities by selling exposed puts and spreads of credit anytime you anticipate a share price to grow. Finally, we're going to be looking at how to utilize puts calls to secure your assets. The design of puts allows them a perfect method to mitigate risk when you're worried about stock downturns in competitive markets.

4.1 The Long-Put Plan-The Downside Play

You gain the opportunity to sell preferred shares after acquisition of a put. Like the futures contract, the call contract is an agreement that determines the cost at that you are allowed to offer the stock, and on which date.

The owner of the long position has the ability to offer the stock at a market price, although he does not have to.

In the other side, once the put is issued, the stock purchase trader has the duty to purchase the product at the market price. Many investors consider it easy to grasp calls, however the placed provides other benefits that are not accessible to the investor with calls. Thus, time is well spent thinking about puts or how to utilize them correctly.

Many of the words used by the alternative are the same based on if they are used for calling or puts. While thinking regarding put options, a put which market rate is greater than all the current market price is alluded to in-the pocket. At-the market also represents a choice that has the same market price and selling price but without money put seems to have a market price greater than the actual stock price. Much as with a put option, there is a greater volatility and more ambiguity in the without money choice role relative to an in-the-money or at-the-money one.

Stock Price at $50

Put Strike Price ($)	Option Price ($)	Time Value ($)	Intrinsic Value ($)	ATM, OTM, or ITM
60.00	10.50	0.50	10.00	In-the-money
55.00	7.00	2.00	5.00	In-the-money
50.00	4.00	4.00	0.00	At-the-money
45.00	2.00	2.00	0.00	Out-of-the-money
40.00	0.50	0.50	0.00	Out-of-the-money

Like we have shown before, just the money paying for an option may be denied to an option purchaser; pure and simple. The benefit risk became potentially limitless for the put option, because there is no ceiling on how far a share price might move. However, there is the cap on an option contract, as a stock's price will never go further than 0. Again, this leaves plenty of space for other stocks to make a return. The same leverage attributes, reduced expense and high future benefits that render purchasing calls appealing often relate to placing options. Just understand that, the enemy of the buyer option is the decay of time. The alternative loses much of its worth when every day goes on, so risky placing purchasing fits well when you operate in a small period of time.

The success graph again for the long-term role clearly shows this plan's minimal danger and massive benefit possibilities:

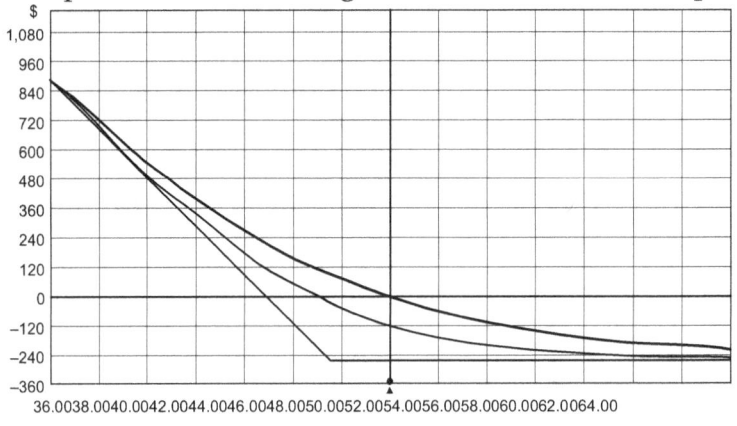

Again, the three lines illustrate how time decay affects the position with the solid line representing the possible outcomes on expiration day. The dashed line represents the theoretical performance of this option halfway between today and expiration, while the dotted line shows what should happen if the stock price were to move to the appropriate price today.

Like with put options, put options are available for many distinct price levels and expiry dates. Since possibilities with various strike action and timeframes react better to stock prices, puts are also necessary in deciding which option method to buy. A lower cost should in no way impact your ability as to which method to buy. Remember, without-money (below stock price) would be the better alternative, and purchasing the others has a reduced chance of winning than buying in- or at-the-money.

Note also that the available period until the expiry date is a crucial consideration in the requirements for the judgment. As far as when the order is delivered, time works against the buyer option. Predict how far you think the expected move in price will took for the inventory to make. Now double this. That would offer you a sensible insight into what expiry month to classify.

Eventually, always be conscious of the actual condition of volatility by gazing at a variance map. This helps you to learn if the options for the stock are traditionally cheap or costly. If the uncertainty implied is really high you might want to avoid purchasing

Faster-in-the-fashion choices. Such options have fewer time premium and they aren't as prone to price shifts. Often, you might want to suggest utilizing a spread to say the chance of uncertainty in that case. The bull put spread, that may be the topic of the next segment, is a strong alternative to holding the purchasing straight while going to speculate on a price decline. While the possible benefits from purchasing places high as a walk-alone approach, never ignore that the related danger is still very high.

4.2 The Bear Put Spread — Speculating of spreads to the downside

A market put spread is another form of playing down business. The relative costs of buying a right over a horizontal debit spread persists for puts almost as accurate as by utilizing calls. Many with bearish market projections will buy puts on a horizontal debit spread, called a bull put spread. A bull placed spread sets the full potential loss and benefit. As soon as the potential profit outweighs the potential loss, you'd recognize the risk valuable.

A bear putting spread entails buying a call options, and then offering the put option further out of the pocket. Its strategy's vulnerability graph is a mirror copy of the horizontal debit distribution, use calls:

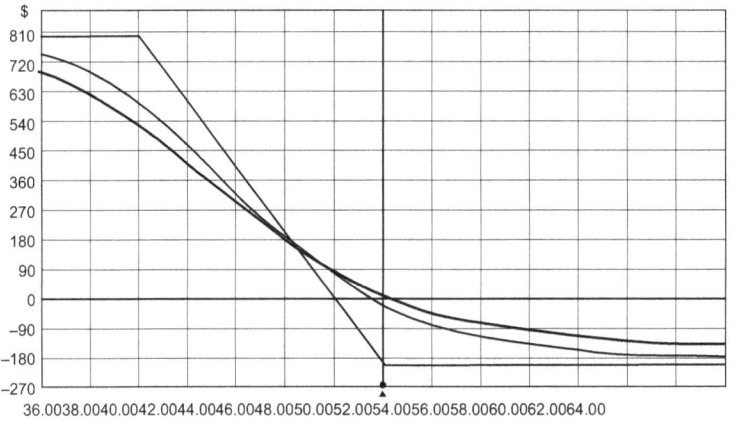

In this case the stock sells for $50 each share right now. You purchase the 40 put and offer the 40 put, to conduct this bull put deal. When you purchase the Fifty put at $3 and market the 40 puts for $1, the actual cost of $200. The worst you will risk on this plan is this $200 expense; nevertheless, the gross benefit is $800 — this same 10-point difference minus the $200 loss.

And even though on termination day the stock was well over $50 the worst you will risk is $200. Unless the stock finishes at $48 on the expiry day, you'll be at the breakeven (regarding the proposed transaction 50-strike value and 2-point cost). You are neither making nor losing any money here. You earn one position in the gap for any dollar under $48 above the $40 each share mark. Their profit from that down prices is corrected at $800. It is a financial benefit of four to one.

The bull put split has the benefit of setting the potential amount but it has the downside of offsetting fixing a maximum income. The bull put spread provides the same features of higher fees and poorer income growth compared to a choice buy. Having that in view, it will not apply to all, but initial option buyers are typically more familiar with this trade's risk level, so embrace the drawbacks in exchange.

4.3 Income Generation-Selling Naked Puts

Another way to produce revenue from puts is simply by offering them directly. Although we mentioned earlier that trading naked puts was an unacceptable, high-risk tactic for most shareholders, trading exposed puts doesn't bear the same form of risk. Typically, with both the short-out strategy just out-of-the-money brings is sold on shares that the shareholder wouldn't mind possessing. If the inventory remains or innovations from around market valuation, the entrepreneur will retain the price if the term ends meaningless.

Such strategy includes reserve, and you will have to deal enough capital in your checking account to "protect" the place in case of activity; hence, such technique is often named the capital-secured placed.

If price decreases for the inventory? The shareholder finally gets allocated the stocks in a certain case, as well as the cost base for his stocks is the put market price minus the discount received. That is why naked bring authors should be ready to purchase the stock before attempting to enter the position.

A stock, for instance, presently trades at $42.50. an empty-money put at a call price of 40 could be auctioned for $2.50, which results in a $250 credit towards your broker account. It doesn't matter what, the $250 is there to carry. Worse, you'll wind up charging $4,000 on every 100 stock options. Deduct a $250, as well as your efficient base is $3,750 for every share, or $37.50. Not such a bad one!

You're thinking that when you go nude with a placed the stock price would increase. It's a positive place because as you purchase calls you have the relevant market targets as you should have. However, the distinction is that call investors have to contend with deterioration of period. They also need market price to rise sufficiently to offset the costs of energy to make a profit. Put dealers on the side have decline in time, and rely on declining time value. Even if stock doesn't change at all, a small put investment may be lucrative. So, a key difference around long calls or short puts is very harder to regularly profit from purchasing calls; selling puts can be fairly easy to consistently profit from. The reason: The value of the time.

The reduction in margin requirement operates against the consumer but to the dealer it is a significant advantage.

When you go nude on a place, you fear purchasing 100 securities at the market price. The put 's owner will only practice it if it's inside the money, meaning you 'd buy the shares at a cost above the market value.

This may not be a bad outcome, as far as you find the price of the strike to be a reasonable price of the product. The sector is full of errors and sometimes there are businesses with undervalued stocks. Getting 100 stocks placed to you in such situations might always be a steal, as soon as you're able to sit out the price.

If you offer a put, you get a coupon that is added to your bank. That is income but, in the incident of exercise, it also special offers the stock price. And if the selling price is $40, then then you offer the put you get a profit of $2,50 the cost base will be $37.50 apiece. The scope of results is outlined in the diagram below. Note that a danger graph is almost the same outline as the call option strategy except that less capital is required for the short put:

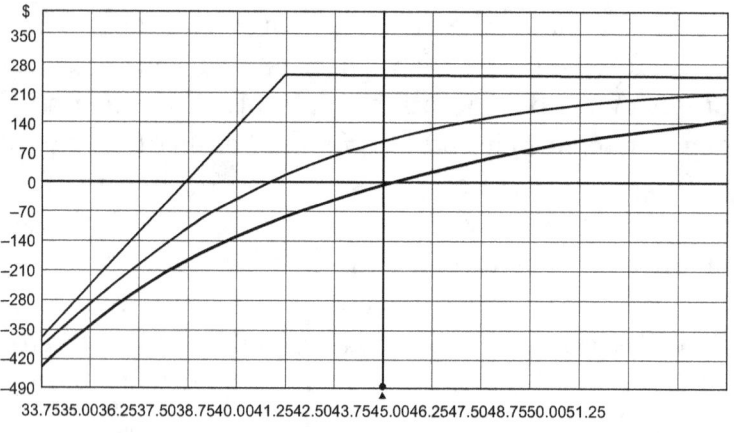

If the stock crosses the $37.50 breakeven point (a margin requirement of 50 minus the premium 2.5 points), the stripped put becomes lucrative. You'll lose a further point for every dollar the inventory falls to below level.

Even then, you should take measures to reduce those loses. For instance, you might instantly sell an income-generating call against common units.

You can give naked starts putting and start preparing for them all to retire; or whether they hold their money quickly also because stock price is rising, you could even close the position — and then continue the cycle over and over again, taking your earnings without endangering the wealth necessary to purchase 100 stock shares. Naturally, in the incident of an exercise, your financial institution would need funds when collateral.

Your perception about the true value of a business may affect your choice to take the exposed put chance. Your danger is theoretically limitless if you go exposed on a bid, since a stock will go up beyond limits; so, when you offer a put, the danger is restricted to the gap between the selling price or zero. In definition, as soon as the firm has resources larger than its debts, the disparity between the market price as well as the tangible market value of the business may be assumed to be restricted to the "actual" risk.

4.4 Utilizing long put to secure the assets

If you keep stock in the investments, you would obviously be worried about the risk that its value can decline. Investors should be especially worried regarding the possible instability of a stock markets. We noted, while addressing the protected call policy, that offering calls offers a limited number of downgrade security.

And purchasing an put to offset the danger of holding assets, also referred to as a defensive put, offers the buyer maximum security against a decline in market price underneath the put's strike point.

In reality this approach is more moderate than simply purchasing stock. There is minimal danger as much as a put is kept towards a stock-position. You know what amount the stock should be priced at.

The two drawbacks are (1) that profits cannot be earned until the product rises past the product and the put total rate, and (2) also that putting has a limited existence. But if the market price increases past the position's overall expense, the opportunity for infinite benefit becomes for an investor.

Owning a security put means buying one put option per each 100 stock securities already held or acquired. Buying a call on stock is equivalent to buying protection, as the buyer charges a fee (the put cost) to cover against a fall of stock value. Regardless of what occurs with the purchase price, the put shareholder is allowed to offer it at the put's market price some period before maturity. The danger graph below shows that this approach has minimal risk and infinite benefit potential:

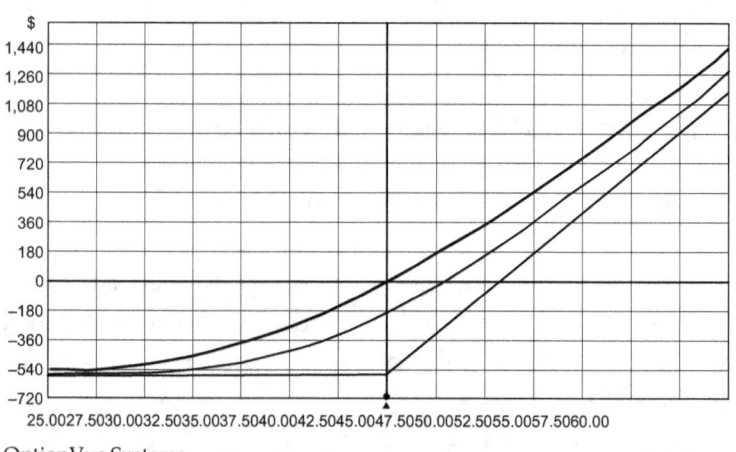

OptionVue Systems

As in the protected call approach, the safe position holder maintains all of the privileges of continued equity ownership over the duration of the put option, until it sells the shares. Unless the selling price of a margin requirement unexpectedly, dramatically declines, a placed seller has the benefit of experience to respond. Know that choice buyer's enemy is time.

The part time benefit of the defensive put would decrease gradually only with passing of

Space, and the decline picks up as the contract alternative hits expiry. But at some point, before it ends, the buyer utilizing the security put is able to resell his stock or his longer put on. For example, if the buyer loses interest over a potential fall in the value in his levered implied vol, the call option could be offered because it has remaining valuation.

When the short position declines and has little interest, there is no need to take action; the buyer can keep their stock. The only step to take is that current business trends already merit stock security. If this is the case, then buy the next one and bring it far out of time. The same rolling options strategy that we previously mentioned with the protected call functions really well with the defensive placed. When the put opens on-the-money, a buyer has 2 option; he may retain the option to sell the common assets at the price of the deal, or merely sell the puts to end it, use the gain earned from either the put to cover the gains from the decrease in market price.

The placed wouldn't have to bought at the very same period as both the product. A common method of utilizing the defensive put technique is to purchase a putting after market price has also risen. If the investor is worried about negative interest rate risk or worries that in the short term the share price can fall down, he may cover his investment losses with a put without needing to hold the company. The placed can still be offered later after the volatility has gone, for what interest it has.

Around now, it would be obvious that through stocks, you will benefit from whether the stock is rising or dropping. Investors prefer to support calls above puts, but puts in a very well-formulated investment strategy will play almost as critical a part as calls.

Both calls or puts may be used solely for betting, profit production or the chance of portfolio positions to be hedged. Take a moment to study the four main options strategies, as each technique or variation develops out of the following:

1. When you're confident you have calls. You assume the price should grow, and you're going to go long and purchase call options. Certain tactics include spreads of bull calls and protected calls if you hold the order.

2. If you're gloomy you have calls. You think the stock should hold within a range of selling or decline in price, so you'll go short or sell call spread.

3. Once you're confident you need holds. If you think the stock would decline, you should go short or sell exposed puts; unless the stock falls, the put gets tired, which can be sold at a benefit or expire. This can only be achieved if you think the valuation of the stock at the market price should be fine. Note, the put will be executed if the market price dropped below yours, then you will have to purchase 100 securities at a strike point. Alternately a bull puts spread can be initiated.

4. When you're gloomy you use holds. When you assume a stock could drop in value, one could go longer and buy spreads or start a short-put spread. If you're right, interest decreases with the put and split. When you own shares, you should even purchase puts in your fund to defend from price declines on shares.

To put it another way, there are many opportunities to purchase or sell stocks.

You may use them to gamble, create sales or hedge risk, based on the individual approach.

Under certain market environments, it cannot make just as much thinking to purchase or sell calls as puts are used accordingly.

Therefore, thinking from both sides — calls or puts — is still smart to identify the tactics that can optimize the gains doesn't matter whatever the aggregate economy is doing. The advantage in stocks is that in every sort in market: rising, down, or flat, calls or put in a right combination, either at the correct time, will yield money. A plan is still possible which will make income. We'll look at a certain basic principles and tactics during the next section, expanding on what we've seen over the last 2 pages.

Chapter 5: Technical and fundamental analysis basics

There are 2 groups used to evaluate stocks and render transactions called basic and scientific analyzes. A quantitative review includes industry analyses and detailed inventories to test as they are oversupplied or overhyped. A quantitative analyst aims at a company's basis for calculating equal worth. Through reflecting at its recent data, technological findings forecast the price of a product. A professional observer knows most how the product is bought by the company, and not only what the product is worth. A professional observer moves through the time and the movement to find out if it should move up or down again.

Comprehending a Bar Chart

A bar map is a basic method for scientific study. The financial assets are stored in bars that are measured as values throughout a specified span of time. Through a bar graph, you can find a stock trend more quickly. In a specified day or time frame, a bar is four rates. This is named the quality counter. The price graph indicates the initial value as a horizontal axis on the left, and the market close as a straight axis on the center. At the height of the bar is the high price, and at the lowest of a bar is the low price reflected.

Candlesticks

A candlestick is a diagram showing the large, small, open, or close each day for a given period for a defense. There're two candlesticks at the foot.

The Bullish Candle would be the one that opens while the near is bigger.

This candle usually has a white and green light. If the near is smaller than the high, the Bearish Candles are.

The middle field indicates the selection of rates to open and shut. As the middle block is put in, the shares fell low than it had opened. Typically, the color is red and black.

Professional Options Evaluation

You need to build ideas and rely on them to be effective with your choices. Please remember the duration a move requires because options reduce interest with the passage of time. Comprehend the choices linked Figures. Learn the proportion of alternatives with an average choice scale. Do not feel too confident. Using approaches of expiry dates to smartly interpret the choices.

Option Greeks

A Greek Option tests the rights exposure to the value of an offer on various probability components.

In a choice price, Differential calculates the market shift. The approximation of a Delta difference for a 1-point shift in an inventory is considered a Gamma. A calculation for an option's time decay is named Theta. Supposed to measure the average variance in the fundamental protection over the last 1 month of closing rates is considered uncertainty. Thanks to interest rate swings, a Rho Greek tests an opportunity amount.

When it relates to technological research, it is necessary to grasp the words. You don't have to learn how they actually function, however. Various coding applications may help you understand their terms and conditions. One of the easiest approaches to benefit from dealing is to know from the experiences of practice.

Put Option vs. call Option

When you purchase protection with contract options, you buy an option to call. When you sell a holding with a contract option you buy the put option

With a more basic sense:

call = Purchase

Create your 6th Sense of Trading

Sell = Put

This is also really tough to recall, which is common because you're a newcomer.

Let me send you only one easy way to know a difference.

If you put a phone call, think about the hand movements.

You raise the phone from the desk towards your ear, if you decide to "call" anyone. And, if your choice is a call, the phone goes "up"-in the same way, you want the value to go.

You "set" the handset down as you're done the chat on the line, and you hang.

call = Order (up)

Sell (Bottom) = Put

I realize that might sound a little dumb, but I'm fairly confident you could also describe it to a five-year-old.

Best Fundamental Options Market Indicator

The simple trend line is among the strongest market movements of trading options.

Investors and traders sometimes say, "Your friend is on the trend! "And" Never deal with the standard!".

When detecting a graph, the price will confirm multiple times in succession for the same tilt/decline. That implies you also have a bullish pattern when you see three rising bottoms mostly on a graph that might be linked to a single node.

When the market continues to sink down a bearish graph, the hope is that the market will rebound, forming a new floor of a trend line. That gives us the chance to buy a protection call alternative.

On the other hand, if you watch three decreasing heights on the chart that can be attached to a couple of lines, then you've got a bearish pattern right before your eyes! If the stock reaches the trendline, that will offer an incentive to buy a call option.

Lines of Trend-options

A typical example of the bearish theme, as shown above. A red indicator shows the bearish pattern of Citigroup. We've got four trend-tops. However, a fourth one suggests that the pattern is breaking away, and we dismiss it as a possible trading incentive. Now let's reflect on the other 3 tops.

In a perfect future, we'll realize at every moment where the demand is heading. In this way, as displayed in the above image, all 3 swing peaks can be traded using a put option.

Given that you now realize how contract options and trends operate, let me incorporate you into the fact now.

As I have mentioned, to validate a bearish pattern, we must find three peaks lying on the same side. Therefore, we remove the first and second bearish trends because they ignore approvals.

The price then produces the 3rd top above the chart, our prerequisite for the bearish trend graph.

It would be a good chance to buy a put option once the stock starts rollover.

The stock declines, and we tend to grab a fall in the share market of 0.5 percent.

The concern is that stocks have a large range of points between the offer and the question. Thus, though you might have a successful stock deal, a .5 percent change would give it a little advantage after commission factoring, and the fact that you have to sell at the price of the auction.

Now let's explore why it's easier to be with a trend than against it. Look at a bearish pattern again on the above chart. Note the arrows green and grey. The green color arrows display the motions of the pattern-the tendencies. The dark arrow represents restorative movements opposite to the trend, leading the price towards new relationships with that pattern or trend. There are two simple explanations of why should you not compete against the pattern in the moves:

- They lead in a slightly smaller market, which changes the cycle shifts.
- They take about the same amount of time to create as the pattern moves.

Options Trading Indicators and Patterns for Increasing Profit

The stock option technical research covers other factors besides trend lines.

Now we are now going to explore a few on-chart resources, which can include actual-time trade signals.

Bulls and bear market:

In the trading sector, nearly every day, you will hear the words "bulls" or "bears" normally used to define market trends.

Since the market sentiment is a big factor that influences your investments, it's necessary to know precisely what words imply and how it all influences you.

KEY TAKEAWAYS

- A bull run is an increasing market, where the market is melodic, whereas a bear place market occurs in a declining economy, where many stocks decline in value.
- While certain investors might be "bearish," most investors are normally "bullish." In the long run, the capital market as a whole has continued to produce high returns.
- Investing in the bear market may be riskier, because many securities lose interest and values are unpredictable.

- Because it is difficult to time the bottom of the market, investors could pull their money off the bear market or sit on the money until around the trend moves in the opposite direction.

What Are Bull and Bear Markets?

The words bull or bearish market is used to explain how financial markets usually do — whether or not they increase or decreases in value. At the very same time, as the economy is decided by the behavior of the buyers, these words often reflect how stakeholders think about the business and the patterns that arise.

In brief, the bull market applies to a growing economy. This is defined by a continuous price rise, for instance, in the money system in the value of the securities of the firms. In these periods, shareholders are also optimistic that the upward trend will persist in the long run. The economy of the nation is usually good in this situation, and job rates are low.

A share market, on the other side, is one in recession, usually dropping 20 percent or more off recent peaks. Share market is constantly falling, going to result in a declining trend believed by shareholders to proceed, which in turn reinforces the negative slide. The economies will usually slow it down after a downtrend, and inflation will increase when businesses continue laying off staff.

Declines and Duration during bear markets.

Characteristics of Bull and Bear Markets

While a state of the bull and market crash is defined by a trajectory of equity values, these are other associated features that shareholders ought to be conscious of. Several of those aspects are listed in the list below.

Demand and Supply for Securities

We see high competition for shares in the bull market and low availability. To put it another way, more people continue to purchase shares, although others are able to sell. As a consequence, share rates should rise as buyers scramble for usable stock.

The same is valid in the bear market since more buyers are attempting to a sale than to purchase. Production is considerably smaller than availability, resulting in a decline in stock values.

Psychology of Investors

Since the conduct of the business is influenced and dictated by how people view this activity, the perception and opinion of consumers influence how the stock will grow or decline. Performance on the share market and psychology of investors is mutually related. Investors actively invest in the expectation of making a return in a share market.

Consumer sentiment becomes pessimistic throughout a bull market as buyers continue pulling their funds out of equity or in fixed-income instruments while they look for a successful change in the financial markets. In brief, the fall in capital market values undermines consumer trust, forcing buyers to pull their funds out of business — which, in effect, triggers a general drop in stocks as outflow rises.

Business and market Change

Since the firms with securities traded on the markets are actors in the broader economy, a capital market, as well as the market, are closely tied together.

A bear run is synonymous with a poor economy because most companies are incapable of making big profits just because customers were not investing nearly sufficiently. Such a drop in earnings, really, has a strong impact on the way investors view the market.

The opposite happens in a share market, when consumers have more resources to invest and are able to buy, which in effect stimulates and grows the economic state of the country.

Keeping account of market changes

The best indicator of whenever the stock is bull and bear aren't only the toe-jerk response of the sector to a single cause, but whether it is doing in the long run. Small shifts reflect either a quick-term pattern or a reversal of the business. It's a prolonged span of time that can decide if you are experiencing a bear or bull market.

Nevertheless, not all of the long market moves may be described as bulls or bears. A business will often go via a cycle of recession when it attempts to find away. A sequence of upward or downside moves in this situation will effectively balance out benefits and loss going in even a balanced market pattern.

It is nearly difficult to schedule the demand exactly.

Where to go in Every Market

The best thing for a trader to do on the bull market is to gain the advantage of increasing rates by purchasing stocks later in the rally, if necessary, and then sell them before they hit their height.

Any will be small and transient throughout the stock market; an individual may usually aggressively and safely participate in further equity at a greater chance of yielding.

Nevertheless, on the bear market, the risk of declines is higher as stocks are constantly losing value, so the end is still not in sight. And if you intend to spend in the expectation of an uptrend, you're likely to miss out before some change takes place. For short sales or healthier assets, like fixed-income instruments, more of the profits can be contained thereby.

The investor can sometimes switch to protective securities, whose success is only moderately affected by evolving market conditions and is hence resilient across both economic recession and prosperity phases. There have been many sectors, such as telecommunications, that are mostly government-owned and services that citizens purchase independent of the economic situation.

Additionally, you will profit from giving a quick place in the bear market, taking advantage of declining rates. There are many ways in which this can be done, such as speculative trading, purchasing reverse ETFs, or purchasing call options.

The Bottom Line

Either bear or bull rates would have a huge impact on your money, and it's a smart decision to take your time and assess whatever the economy is doing before creating the investing choice. Note the financial sector has still reported a good performance in the long run.

Volume Indicator

The volume predictor is an instrument that is displayed underneath the market activity.

It reflects market changes in red in both downward price movements.

The irony about this is that quantity also has a strong connection to price, and that is the core of stocks.

The variability is always strong when the prices are rising, or the inventory is rising. The uncertainty is small, while sales are weak, so stock is within a range of exchange. Take a look at a photo below it, and you'll see I meant by:

Options and Volume

This is Yum Brands' 1-minute graphs. At the lower end of a chart, we also see a metric for volumes.

You note at the start of the map the YUM stock choice options on very small volumes of trade. And at 11:30 its amounts of YUM trade raise significantly within 15 min. That is because the preferred stock just has a 0.4 percent instant spike!

Conclusion – While the amounts are large, moving movements tend to be on the marketplace to grab.

Indicators of Chart Pattern

Graph trends are key to equity option statistical research. Chart trends are mathematical statistics that the market behavior on a graph produces. Such estimates highlight significant market fluctuations that could be tradable.

There are two simple trends in the chart:

• Trend Consistency Chart Trends: These are just the shapes that form during cycles, which indicate that the pattern should proceed along the same lines. Let me give you many of the more familiar trends in the pattern continuity table.

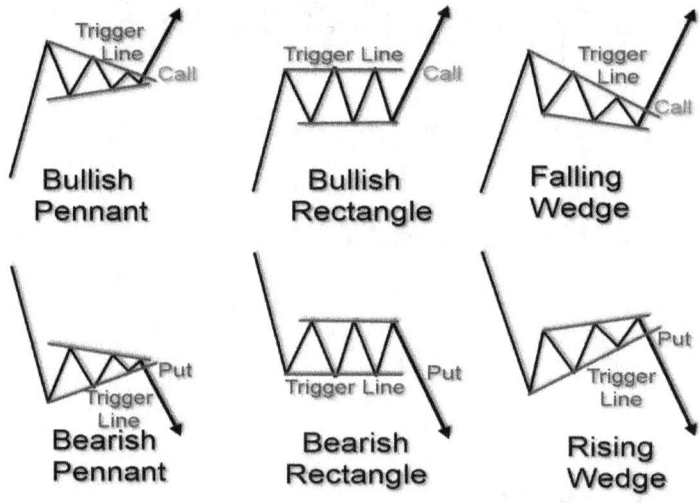

Continuation Chart Patterns

Above, you have six from the most exchanged trends of share options in the continuity table. The above three trends react to a continuity of the optimistic trend. They become mirror copies of the bottom four ones, pointing to a continuity of bearish cycles.

Every pattern has a triggering line. That is a line that is split by a price after confirmation of the design. This way, once the price hits the switch, it's a warning for market entry. So, an ask option should be used to trade the outer three trends. Conversely, the lower 3 trends can be sold with a put choice.

When testing every one of these trends, we predict a price change compared to, at minimum, the scale of the specific pattern.

• Trend Reverse Map trends: These are the statistics produced at trend end. They mean that the pattern will be at its end in this sense and that the price is likely to shift directions. Look at the photo below.

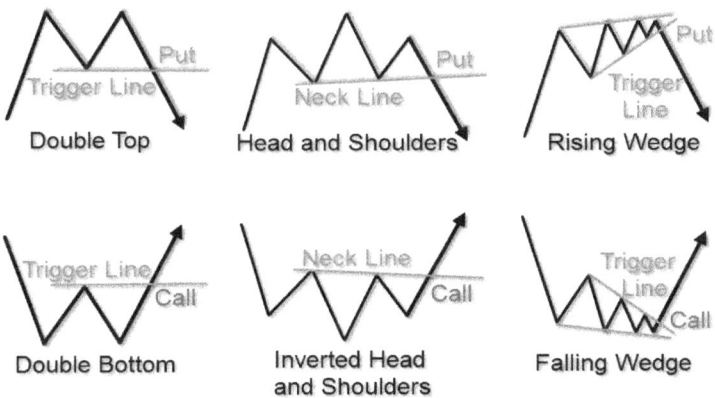

Chart Patterns Triggers

These are all the six reversal map trends most widely exchanged on share options. Keep in mind that the outer band reflects the smaller group images.

The growing pattern in the chart does have a trigger thread. If you trade chart analysis for the heads or shoulders, this model is known as "neck." It's under the heads and shoulders, after all, correct? When a price breaks each pattern's trigger section, we anticipate a price change in the pattern direction. Additionally, the scale of the planned change would possibly be normally as large as the trend itself.

Remember that the increasing and dropping wedges perform the function of a cycle of pattern continuity or trend reversing.

How is that possible?

I'll give you a quick law to recognize: there's always bearish opportunity in the increasing sideways, and the dropping wedge does have the bullish opportunity. The dropping wedge in the first situation falls after a bumpy pattern. Because the dropping spike has positive power, in that case, it plays a function of continuity.

Unless the dropping wedge falls on a bearish run, however, while it has bullish power.

Such laws often relate, but in a reverse way, to the growing wedge.

Chapter 6: Modified and advanced concept strategies

Options will liberate you from conventional financial strategies' uncertainty. Now that you're firmly grounded throughout the fundamentals of trading options, we'll implement a few of the many more modern concepts or strategies. While we're not going to go through this in as much depth as we named or swing trades, it's crucial that you understand the wide variety of options open to you and start familiarizing yourself with a few of the principles that all good traders in options need to learn.

We're going to start by spending time looking in much more detail at three key concepts: option valuations, volatility, and also the Greeks. An absolute valuation segment will provide you an analysis of the characteristics which decide what an option's "fair value" is. The volatility segment describes its value, and also brings you to historical variance charts that enable you to see a stock's actual volatile condition. The next idea we will stare at is that how option investors calculate the intensity of the price of an option to variations in different factors, and so we will describe idiomatic phrases such as Gamma, Delta, Vega, and Theta; otherwise recognized as "the Greeks."

Ultimately, we should look briefly at a variety of advanced approaches, clarify how they are built, demonstrate its risk/reward value with a chart, and address the most appropriate demand forecasts and business environments under which they should be. There are three main directions to the market: upwards, downwards, or sideways. Once you put a deal, it's necessary to determine the future demand movement. Of starters, you might purchase calls, sell calls, or purchase the stock themselves, because the price is through. Have you got any further choices? Hey. In a large variety of approaches, you will mix shorter and longer options with the implied vol. Such approaches are structured to minimize the exposure while profiting from different demand perceptions or market trends.

6.1 Options of pricing — What is a "fair" cost for such an option?

In 1973, Fisher Black or Myron Scholes launched an option-pricing pattern, named a Black-Scholes method. This pricing offered the first realistic way for options investors to determine easily what a choice "would be" worth. Although changes have been made and over the years, a version of this approach is normally at the core of most pricing strategies for choices today. We're not going to go into the numerical specifics, but the primary inputs in the model seem to be Price, Time, Volatility (preferably, the long-term volatility of the stock), the interest rate, or Dividend payments (payable over the option period).

A successful valuation software system of options will integrate all these factors into the price structure and reveal potential values for every alternative today and in the future as well. Using the model, the algorithm will create graphs that represent the potential actions of every option transaction at some stage in the future, including those you see from this novel. If you have industry options, knowledge and are good at doing simple arithmetic into your mind, you will need to utilize a pc to display such graphs or assist you in making your decision.

We have also looked at the effect on the valuation of an option the market price and period have. Whether the pricing of an option influences, the value of the implied vol is relatively clear. It is, therefore, a relatively simple idea to recognize that the valuation of an option declines gradually with the passing of time, but you should be mindful that option values will not drop linearly: the moment discount erodes more quickly when the choice reaches the expiry date. Interest levels and distributions are generally just a small impact on an option's quality. But it's worth the time it takes to look at a little further detail at the initial input-volatility.

Ways to combat anxiety about forex trading and build trust:

Whether you're studying how to do stock trading for the very first time feeling uncertain of where to continue, then you've been throughout the market for a moment but recently hit with such the number of failures and resulting personality-doubt, there will be plenty of strategies you can use to harbor trust while trading.

Being a profession based on circumstances of volatility, this form of trading will end in forex investors feeling overjoyed one day after a good victory, and incredibly poor the next day after a major loss. Because of the inherent volatility of the business, it's important that you try to build a solid mindset to assist you in forming a new career in a foreign currency environment. Therefore, to assist you to do so, we're revealing 3 currency trading pieces of advice sure to support you fight anxiety about trading and develop your market confidence.

Process Focus

We're going to be the one to say this; foreign currency markets remain unpredictable. Although there are, of course, a variety of methods that you can use to help you forecast price trends, there is no easy way to tell whether you should prepare to see a gain or a loss. As a consequence, in difficult cases, you have to be mindful of the trade phase because if opposed to depending on the returns on investment, because that will help you to feel nervous and worried as a consequence.

So, it's important with day-to-day dealing that you don't always bother yourself with the future result of your transactions. Rather, you ought to try to focus on checking off certain facets of a forex plan – and besides, if you have implemented one about your own laws, that's been a victory in itself! Although this method will not particularly assist you in seeing instant outcomes, it is an important exercise to construct life-discipline and will assist make you sound more hopeful in the long run.

Be positive

It will come as no shock for you that performance and trust intertwine. However, how many positive people are familiar with who has a totally negative behavior to challenges, or get a hard time feeling bad as problems occur, rather than solving the problem they face? We would not have expected that many.

Even so, while losing trades is normal, it's the way you treat with those circumstances that will make you the currency exchange trader. Consequently, in a way to get rid of fear and develop your credibility, it is important that you think positively – avoiding bad emotions over how many you wasted since they first emerge and talking about the steps you tried to take to get anywhere instead.

For starters, ask oneself: what worked well this way around instead of, startlingly, what might you have accomplished differently in the case of a specific scenario turning up at some point? Recognizing the optimistic as well as the bad can make you feel a bit more comfortable about new trading environments, as you are better equipped in the awareness that you have handled similar circumstances in the old days – or if you can go through that, then you could get over that now.

Practice and practice more!

Certainly, if you'd like to know more about the currency market, you'll have to train over and over again. And besides, boxing hero Muhammad Ali certainly doesn't deserve his name but managed to gain 56 of the 61 battles without professional experience, preparation, several knockouts, and a lot of self-confidence.

As a forex investor, you're not going to able to guess how the economies will shift and what hits are over the first door waiting on them. But, to have a likelihood of winning and develop trust to address such situations while they are managed by you, you have to brace mentally for any potential situation – building a completely tested forex plan willing to start every potential outcome. Only after that do you be comfortable in executing highly risky trade centered on how you've come to understand from past circumstances.

To exchange forex with faith, you'll have to know that performance and trust go hand in hand. Firstly, be sure you trust in oneself, and pursue your investing or risk reduction methods – you'll quickly realize that you're on the way to having the number of gains exceed the losses.

6.2 Understanding Volatility-Critical Value for Traders in Options

Earlier it was noted that uncertainty seems to be the most overlooked of the main factor affecting the pricing model. We don't want to have the mistake anywhere. Uncertainty is indeed a vital concern when dealing with options.

Each asset seems to have quiet times when it has cheap options, as well as volatile duration when it has expensive options. Skilled option investors are sometimes mindful of present rates of uncertainty in contrast to the background information. They look at past liquidity graphs to gain a certain viewpoint. The diagram below displays a comparison chart:

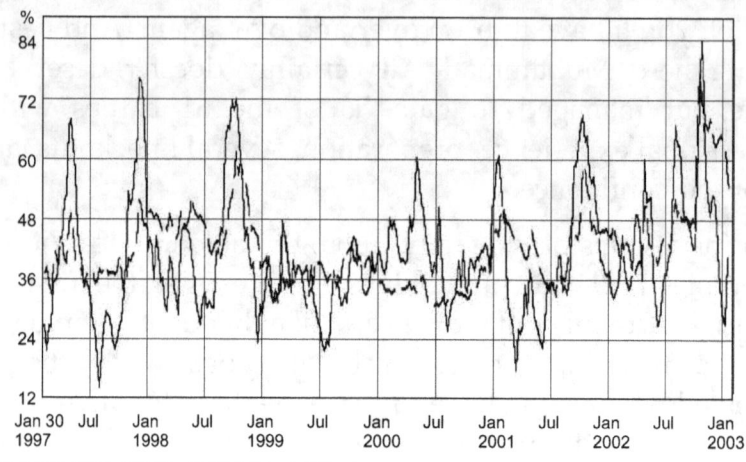

Averages	3 weeks	6 weeks	10 weeks	1.5 years	3 years	4.5 years	6 years
Statistical	32.0%	35.6%	42.1%	46.5%	42.7%	41.0%	40.3%
Implied	60.3%	62.3%	63.7%	48.8%	42.9%	41.4%	42.2%

Option Vue Systems:

The liquidity chart shows two lines-one for quantitative uncertainty (SV) and one for backwardation (IV). The good SV path reflects the total volatility of routine price volatility in the stock at every point. Numerical volatility is sometimes referred to as "historical" variance, but they prefer the statistical definition, as the liquidity charts provide historical details both for SV or IV. The tumbled IV path reflects the minimum volatility implied to the stock for each point. In other terms, a Sv line tells you the stock's true volatility, whereas an IV line displays you the uncertainty indicated by the stock's options prices. Typically, they would be relatively similar away. If they are not, the cost of the options would indicate that it does not reflect the true volatility of a stock. At the lower of the map is a useful chart that sums up the cumulative SV and IV over various time intervals.

Liquidity graphs often help to decide what variance is "natural." If current uncertainty transiently goes far greater or lesser than the past, this can assist you in creating profit. It may also be helpful for detecting price trends you should reap the benefits of. A stock's price will vary from null to zero. Volatility can't extend too far. Since moving to high, the buyer can still depend on uncertainty gradually dropping to usual rates. This parameter is known as the "mean volatility reversal trend." this could take days with months from anywhere, but eventually, volatility every time returns to the center ground.

In general, implicit volatility continues to grow as share prices fall and falls as stock demand rises. The reason for this is that falling share prices entail higher uncertainties risk. This results in an increased compensation market toward possible losses, implying a stronger requirement for call options. Such a market brings forces perceived elevated uncertainty. Rising equity values, but at the other end, imply less confusion and consequently less competition for long positions leading to lower volatility. This expertise is of great use to buyers' options. For example, although the valuation of a call may rise only with the market price, the price-volatility finding indicates the contract will sacrifice some of its prices due to a dropping price. However, it's great news for putting investors because put will appreciate in demand from double impact of dropping rates and rising uncertainty.

Many times, there will be near alignment between expected variability and actual variability, although on certain occasions, one will rise well over the certain. You will also be conscious of recent news regarding the shares that you sell. Incidents can occasionally overwhelm patterns of historical data. Be very careful of the method where there is high implemented volatility, and extremely low graphical volatility. Figure out if an acquisition bid seems to be on the cards. These agreements often defrost stock of the company for a moment in a small spectrum of trading. Meanwhile, due to the extreme probability of a drastic improvement in the contract, that options will bear large premiums. Overall, unexpected incidents may be risky for traders in options-so be cautious!

6.3 Time ranges — Mixing options with various expiry dates

It is pointed to it as a date spread, and time propagates, when you merge choices of each kind but with specific expiry dates. We listed one illustration earlier that we spoke of utilizing LEAPS also as a stock replacement. The spread included purchasing a call from LEAPS but instead offering a call for a short period. Timetable spreads will also protect all choices for the short term. If both options' market price is the same, it is considered a vertical split. You might buy a call in June, for instance, and offer a call in February at the same market price. This is a danger graph showing the future danger/reward account for that trade:

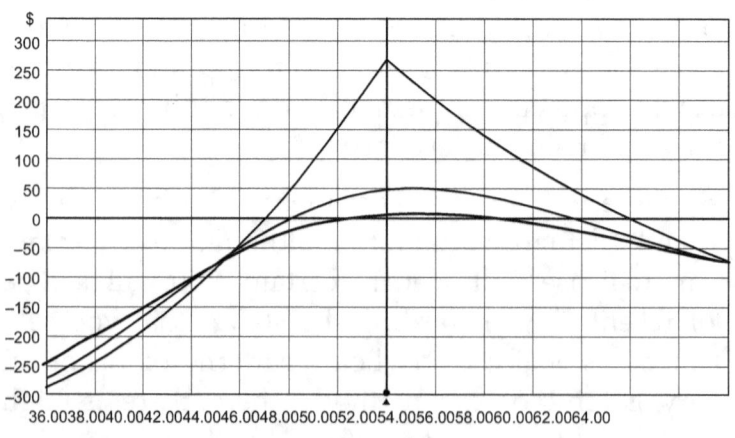

OptionVue Systems

If you will see, this deal gains at least before the short choice ends while the market price holds within a selling range. You're the greatest possible outcomes when a share price ends on an expiry day, essentially at a brief option's market price. The exact shape and placement of the "tent" rely on which quality is used for the attack. You are beginning to think for 2 outcomes throughout this trade. Second, the short alternative would expire empty, or you may close this at again. Third, that even the long right that ends later would be lucrative until expiry. That technique works because the time premium drops from the request in February, and the demand instead goes up until the call ends in June. You should, of course, still shut down the whole place on the short choice expiry date. Perhaps you might "rollover" over the next termination month, and offer a short contract.

A variable split is a daily spread variance where both the expiry date and the current value for shorter and longer options are specific. For instance, you could wish to buy a call from June 50 and sell a call from February 55. In fact, this exchange could have a bearish account, as the quality graph illustrates:

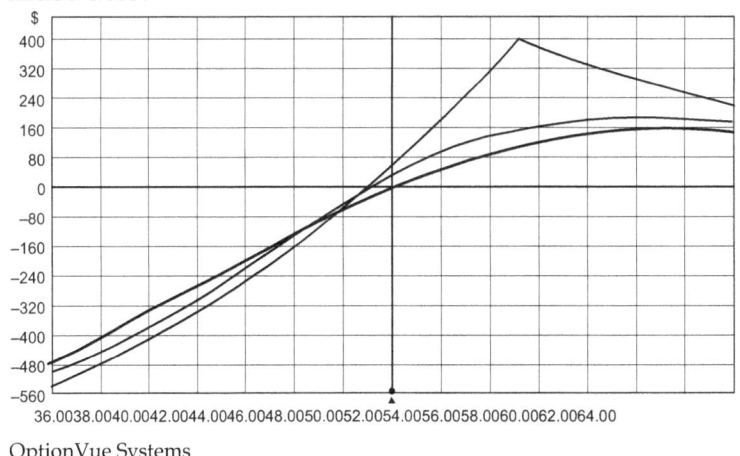

OptionVue Systems

The highest potential benefit is then if the market trade expires on expiry day at precisely the long option's strike trade. You can easily see, though, that it is a positive dimensional investment as well. If the cost of a strike rises, otherwise you'll lose capital. However, if the market price rises, a relatively large variety of this exchange becomes lucrative. Using put for downward betting operates a certain approach almost as well. You could perhaps buy a put-on June 50, for instance, and sell the put-on October 45.

Timetable spreads can be noted to be particularly prone to shifts in variability. A rise invariance will significantly improve the benefit (the longer, much further-out choice would raise the premium greater than the neighboring short choice). By the very same time, a significant decrease in the value for such trades may be catastrophic. So, be cautious not to join this form of trading in the stock in which the existing implied level of uncertainty is at a record peak.

6.4 Spreading the Percentage — Purchasing and trading unequal options

Every spread approach we have seen up to this stage has included equal sums of both shorter and longer options. And there are even ratio approaches, where there is no equal lot of extra options or short choices. One effective technique on the ratio is called spreading the back. It's great for occasions where you're planning a major price change, but at the same time, you 're conscious you may be incorrect, and no step is going to happen.

A back split is created by shortening a fairly close-the-money contract and instead of buying a greater amount of the same form of options at a more out-of-money strike point. The most popular ratio is one to two, so you will aim to pick the stocks in a manner that the choice you 're shorting takes in a profit that meets the expense of the rights you 're purchasing, contributing to no net income, or only a slight profit to your balance.

The back-split call ratio is a hedged positional position in which we intend to benefit from a fast-upward shift while covering our drawbacks. If the market price increases, you'll profit from both the upward change of demand — comparable to a longer call place. If the assumptions turn up to be incorrect and the economy is turning towards you, you would be structured in such a manner that you can either not fail, or perhaps step into a slight profit sector.

Because your net long shares, the opportunity for benefit is infinite, and because the selling of the more costly options accounts for an option they own, if all legs fail worthlessly, it costs everyone nothing. The rear spread's short leg also helps to reduce time-decay as a concern. Nonetheless,

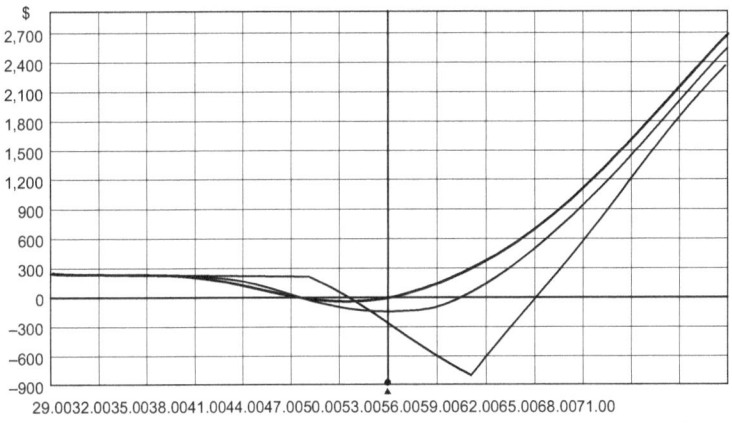

OptionVue Systems

There's one catch here. There is still a market zone in which the back spreading makes a loss, so it occurs when the stock passes by just a small portion in the wanted direction. But it requires time to establish the full cost, and the probability can sometimes be balanced by utilizing long-term alternatives. So, if the anticipated-for major move fails in a timely manner to eventuate, you can shut the situation for a slight loss.

Remember that if you are bullish, the backed spread can be built very well with slips, and act to the label back spread in a mirror way.

6.5 Combining Calls and Puts in a Single Strategy

The trading approach choice is named as a straddle. Through this technique, both a put and a call on the very same inventory are mixed. Straddles may be marketed for sales, or purchased for investment. Let us assume, for instance, that a share is trading at $50 a share right now. You will offer the 50 and 50 calls along with the expiry date and also get $3 mostly on call and $3 mostly on put as well. Six dollars up, you get a $600 credit for your balance. The inventory could shift $6 in any path by day of expire

And you'd break up. In any direction, the stock shifted further than that. Otherwise, you'd start losing capital. Let's look at one quick straddle's cost/benefit profile:

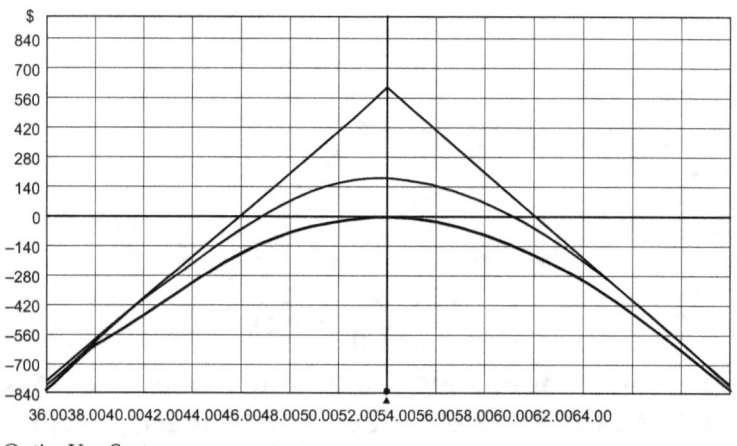

OptionVue Systems

Any or all of these choices can, at any time, be closed to benefit. The major benefit of this exchange is also that time interest arrives from both ends, enabling you to make a profit from all calls and place them as you end. For instance, that means the share price is not going too far in any way. The small straddle is intended to produce profits on inventories that stay within a very limited range of trading. The drawback is that the necessary margin would likely be very high.

The stock had been right at a strike price in a previous case, which is optimal for a straddle. That's because both calls, as well as the put, offered overall premium, are 100 percent -time interest. And all the interest, by death, would evaporate. The only interest remaining on the expiry date is the residual meaning either in the call or in the put. And, in the straddle, you realize that one side would expire uselessly; as far and they got the similar strike price, a call cannot have inherent value and place it on the same stock.

In a short straddle, you encounter a lot of danger, given the likelihood that a stock will shift dramatically in one path or another. The price you earn for the selling of all options only mitigates the danger within a limited range of trading. And, in case of major market moves, you show yourself, either upwards or downwards. You might offset the risk by purchasing options from both sides at a high strike price and reducing the possible loss, but it will also minimize the future benefit from the compensation you got when you first sold the puts and calls. The small straddle could be a risky maneuver, so to protect your place, you need to be prepared to move fast.

Another option of using straddles will be to go far. You 'd purchase calls with large straddle and sets them at a similar strike point. Although there is less chance of failure from a market change in the long straddle, it's also tougher to make again. The share price will rise fast enough with one path or another to (1) cover the premium expense of all options or (2) eliminate the interested decline due to decay over time. And if the combined cost of the call as well as a put is 6 cents, use the same values we utilized in the earlier study, the market price will have to go up or down $06 only to break out, so it's got to jump further than that to earn a profit. The reliability chart of a lengthy straddle is shown in the figure below:

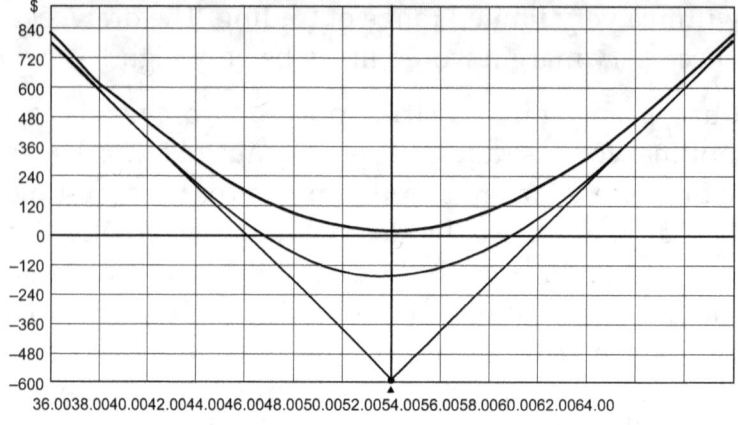

OptionVue Systems

The picture shows clearly how big a buying pressure you have to earn a profit on that trade. So, if the share price doesn't move, other timelines illustrate the constant reduction in worth because of a time delay.

Calling and placing needn't always be on a similar strike speed. The risk/reward balance of the exchange may be changed by changing the strike rates. Once I first began selling stocks, it was just considered a straddle, regardless of longer what a strike costs, whether you purchased or traded a call as well as a put around the same time. But as time passed, it has become common to call trade a "strangle" if they had distinct strike prices. The terms or gestures used during the trading options change with time.

But those risk bar charts do not display the entire story. Previously in this section, when we mentioned the impacts of fluctuation on the worth of an option, we noted that alterations in volatility impact call and put in a same way.

That says, straddles are particularly susceptible to variability. In addition, certain traders' futures, or volatility investors, using straddles to reap the benefits of anticipated volatility shifts, rather than size. A rise invariance will benefit a long straddle, yet a shorter straddle would damage, and a visa vs. It is, therefore, prudent to make heavy straddles on shares at low rates of high vol and sell shorter straddles on shares at historic highs of high vol (selling costly options).

Let's pass on and have a peek at two markets mixing puts, calls, and stock: the protected combination and the collar contract.

6.6 Buying stock with Covered Combine inexpensively

When the choices are really costly, seeking a way to market them makes sense. Covered reading is a great way, but if the share price drops all of a sudden, you also lose. How if you were able to buy some safe investments at a price underneath their present level? The combination that's protected lets you do exactly that.

The combination technique used is a protected call plus a limited put. In order to purchase the product, selling the of out-of-the-money request to shape the protected paper, and a put placed at a market price in which you are able to purchase some of the stock's assets would earn a strong premium. The shorter puts are called a naked choice because if the market price drops below the put's market price, then you will have to purchase more securities and be allocated. You just have to be ready for that.

Since the mix protected has you offering products, this approach is ideal for high-option pricing seasons. Let us take a look at one case. We may offer a long position for $3 at the 60 prices for a portfolio currently priced at $50, which offers us

Three points of defense against the downside. In other terms, until we suffered a loss, the inventory could collapse to $47. Add to this than the $4 benefit accessible by offering a put at 45 strike prices. Wherever the market price falls, the benefit earned from the put sale lets us purchase the initial 100 stock shares for Four points lesser. Taking into account the proceeds of the puts and calls around each other, we are essentially buying a stock of $43. This is under the actual market cap of $7.00! In the estimate below the whole trade is photographed:

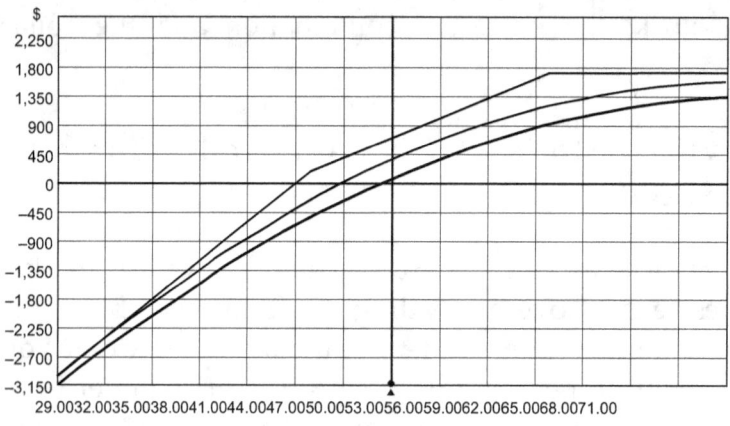

OptionVue Systems

If the stock fell below $45, it will definitely be given our (presently) on the-money putting and have to purchase an extra 100 stock shares at $45. So, the very first 100 stocks cost us $43 a day and the 2nd $45 each. Which implies we get an average cost of $44 for 200 units. Not big a deal, taking into account that stock's current price is $50!

What is the trap, then? The pass is that if a stock keeps falling, we 'll lose $200 per level on our 200 stock shares. If the stock then soars, instead, we will raise $1,700 or no more, because our profit profits are limited by the call options. Therefore, in fact, our income is small, but our possible loss is far larger; that is to say, any cost below $35.50 would result in a loss of more than $1,700.

6.7 Trade in the Collar: Hedging the portfolio for so little to more

The best way to secure the profits in a portfolio is to purchase a safe put without ever trading it. It also has the benefit of enabling you to retain all of the profits if the stock rises, so if the demand declines, you are protected. Cost is the downside of the approach. When the market price goes up, buyers continue to grumble at the placed premium cost. Many people actually avoid purchasing the puts over a lengthy bull market.

One method you can now get from around the expense of insurance against the drawback is by utilizing a collar deal. A collar trading is a shield confining the exposure to a given set. To build a collar exchange across a stockholder, you purchase one call option to every 100 stock shares; you have to defend the stock from a price drop. So, you offer call options to help compensate for the puts. It's also possible to build what is considered a "costless" collar on certain options, where the money earned by selling calls pays for purchasing the puts absolutely. Whatever collar commerce does is to lock you into a band of protected prices. You are safe if the stock falls below the put's strike price, but you lose all gain over the call's strike price.

You may put a collar trade, in the same manner, you buy the product. When you have intangible profits to cover, it's a really useful technique too. Let's look at a scenario of a stock trading currently at $55. You may buy a $2.50 July 45 put and sell a $2.50 July 65 call. The stock would charge you $5,500 per 100 shares, but the two options eliminate the debit or credit, meaning that the options pay you to zero.

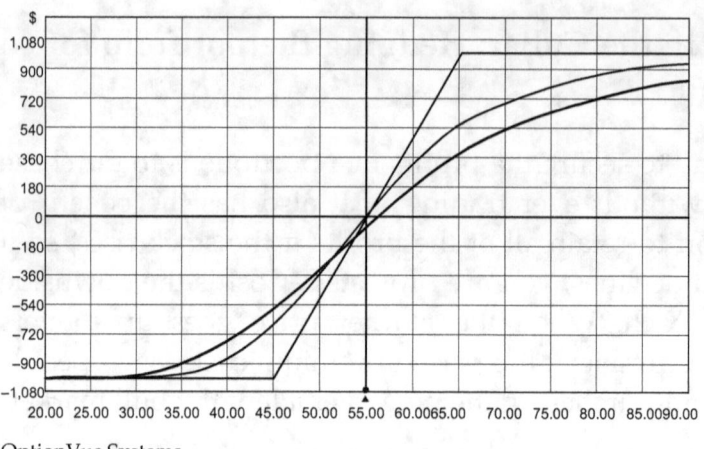

OptionVue Systems

Now, during today's or the July deadline, a variety of items could occur to the share price.

- The share price may run from $45 to $65. Both rights would expire useless throughout this situation, but you already hold 100 stock securities. If the options cost you little, you're no good or worse off than actually owning the stock (although at night you've gone to sleep a little easier).
- By an expiry date, the share price may fall below $45. Under this scenario, not knowing how much the market value drops, you may risk up for $1,000. It is the "stand" the bell creates. In contrast, if the share price falls to $40, if you can only buy shares, you'd had also lost $1,500! And with the stock alone, the losses could go on rising.
- Share prices can rise above $65. When this occurs, the securities will be priced at $65, and it doesn't matter how much the price of the stock rises. For all those 187 days, that will earn you an income of $1,000, an 18 percent yield (annualized 35 percent).

When the stock price drop drastically, will you make changes to maximize the overall productivity of a position? Needless to say! The change consists of selling the long put, purchasing back a short call, and then placing a pearl bracelet on cash. If the based on the market price has dropped, a gain will be made responsible for the enhanced sell, but another benefit will be made in the short position buy. The latest collar would then begin to cover the sideways place at the present level, which would make gains if the inventory were to go higher. The current collar won't need much if there is any extra cash in your wallet because selling call funds the put's expense for the current collar. It typically makes perfect sense to suggest such an improvement if the market price has fallen by about 20 percent or so. It's such a good plan! If a stock market crashes, it helps you can hold in your gains, hold a longer-term positive stance, and have reduced risk.

Trading options include continuous trading and share price tracking. You will only learn whether to behave to boost revenue or reduce damages by paying any attention. Most methods of options — particularly its mixtures — must be decided to open, and then disregarded. But while certain items with choices are feasible, this doesn't necessarily imply they have to be achieved. Predictability raises the price, and the bigger the fees are, the more and more rights you sell. And it could be feeding through your dividends. The ways to utilize equity options offer exciting options for (1) mere investment, (2) income-generating, and (3) risk-hedging. But equity incentives were not only viable choices. In the concluding section, we'll explain how to utilize strategy research, options the interest of which is calculated by a portfolio basket. Eventually, we'll explore what might be some of the last moves when you continue trading options.

Chapter 7: Links and steps to activate with your broker

Investing profitably enables you to use the same broker company that conforms with your financial priorities, training qualifications, and personal style. Choosing the right online financial manager that fits your requirements, particularly for new shareholders, may make a big difference with an interesting new investment portfolio and severe loss.

Although there are no entirely convinced-fire means of guaranteeing returns on investment, there is indeed a way of setting oneself help and protect by choosing the investment account that better fits your description. In this tutorial, we'll dissolve anything that you can search for in your perfect broker, of the apparent to something not-so-accurate (as how simple it really is to get help from a real person when you really need it).

Key points

- Exposure to the markets is cheap and easy due to a number of retail brokers operating online portals.
- Various online traders are tailored for a particular category of the customer — from lengthy-term buy-or-hold newcomers to professional, successful day trades.
- picking a right broker online needs any proper research to have the best out of your investment. Obey the measures and recommendations to pick the right one in this post.

1: Remind yourself about your desires

Take a minute to zero in on what is really essential to you that in a trading site, before they start pressing on broker advertising. Based on the financial goals and also where people are along the investing learning process, the solution may be subtly different.

When you're just heading out, features such as simple educational tools, detailed glossaries, fast access to help personnel, and the opportunity to learn trades until you actually play with actual money might be priorities.

If you already have certain investing expertise into your belt but are ready to get ambitious, you may like more strong-level information or interpretation-based tools published by active traders and experts, and a broad range of simple and technical info.

A genuinely professional trader, maybe someone who has already carried out dozens of trades but also looking for a different broker, would offer preference to sophisticated charting tools, dependent order rights, and the right to trade futures, bonds, shares, and specified-income instruments, and stocks.

Be frank on what you see on the investing path right now, where you'd like to go. Would you try to create an IRA and 401(k) retirement plan and concentrate on passive assets that will produce tax-free money? Would you like to look down your nose in day-trading and don't know how to get started? Would you prefer the thought of designing your entire portfolio and tailoring it, or are you able to hire a specialist to make sure it's done right?

Relying on the direction you follow, there could be even more queries that you may need to address when you acquire knowledge and develop your objectives. Beginning with any of these four key criteria for now, though, will help you decide which one of the brokers features we will cover below would be most relevant. We also provided some test questions below each wider subject to help keep the analytical impulses flowing:

1. You 're an aggressive or inactive investor, in general? Want to be very hands-on to do day- and swing-trades? Can you

finally see yourself abandoning the 9-to-5 routine and being a maximum-time entrepreneur? Or, then, are you searching for a few good assets with little to no day-to-day contact to carry for the longer term?

2. How many do you understand? Which sort of trades do you like to carry out? Will you be the sort of shareholder that understands what the like to do and only wants a forum that allows trading simple and fast, or would you like the broker with such a broader arsenal of tools to help you look for chances? Which kind of stocks are you targeting? Stocks, ETFs, mutual funds? Would you want to exchange stocks, derivatives, or fixed-income instruments even if you're more sophisticated? What are retailing margins? Want exposure to contingent orders, longer trading hours, and currency trading choices?

3. Want to help? What type? Would you go towards the DIY road, learn how to view charts or financial details in order to discover and carry out your own trading, or would you like to employ a pro? How are you in the learning process because you decide to go for it yourself? Which kind of tools are you supposed to use to draw on your understanding? Need quick access to help workers, or will you discover what you have to know via online learning resources? Would you want to conduct trades remotely, or do you like to dial in and get a broker and support you with a procedure?

4. What are the targets? In what do you invest? Why do you choose for an investment? Seek to supplement your daily salary to boost your existing living standards? Was there some special case or cost you'd like to fund? Would you plan to potentially be your main source of revenue for this? Are you seeking to set up private pensions, and if so, do you still want a retirement plan, or would you like to start a new one through your fund of choice?

Such queries are not replied incorrectly. Be honest about how many of your important movements, energy, and struggle you are willing to put in the investments. Over time, your answers will shift, and that is good. Will not try to predict any of your desires and priorities for all the remainder of your career. Just start right now, with what you have right now.

2: Narrow down your area

Now that you're having a clear understanding of what their investment objective is or what essential services you are going to start looking in your perfect brokers, it is time to winnow down your choices a little bit. Although there are many brokerage elements that might be more essential to some shareholders than others, there are also some things that should have any reliable brokerage online. Checking the simple needs for such a wide variety of choices is a perfect way to easily narrow the spectrum.

Stock Broker and Trust Regulation

Is the courier a Financial Investor Security Company (SIPC) member? Usually, there should be a form of description or warning at the end of the homepage. The company can be easily looked up on the SIPC platform.

Is the broker a part of the regulatory body for the financial sector (FINRA)? It should be noted very clearly in a location that is easy to find. You can view brokerages on the website of FINRA's Brokerage Check.

Is the company protected by the National Federal insurance Company (FDIC) as it sells checking or investment accounts, or all other investment items? Investment plans – such as securities or mutual funds invested in commodities, shares, futures, and insurance policies – are not covered by FDIC, since the security of the assets cannot be assured. Moreover, if the company sells CDs, Term deposit Deposit Arrangements

(MMDAs), banking accounts, or investment accounts, the FDIC will completely back them up.

What form of protection do they have to cover you in the event that the business fails? As a participant of a SIPC, the business will provide policies with a cap of at minimum $500,000 per client, with $250,000 reserved for cash complaints. If the corporation conforms to the consumer rights Rule, further coverage should also be provided over and above the SIPC's minimum standards.

Is there some sort of protection toward fraud? Does the business compensate you for fraud-related losses? Be sure that you double test what the company expects of you will be reimbursed. Figure out whether you need to have some evidence or take clear measures for your own safety.

What is it the new consumers assume? Start looking for brokerage user feedback online, utilizing terms such as "insurance allegation," "fraud defense," and "customer care." Obviously, online comments can usually be viewed with a pinch of salt – certain people feel like moaning. Moreover, when there are many users from various places that are all voicing the same claim, then you might want to further examine.

Online monitoring and account safety

It's crucial to know well how your data is secured by a brokerage.

Does it provide two-factor protection on the broker website? Can you get the choice in response to your key to triggering a protection feature? Responding to security requests, obtaining special, moment-sensitive keys through email or text, or utilizing a data security keys that fit in your USB, may be popular.

Which kind of software is the broker employing to keep the data secure? Find out how the broker utilizes "cookies" or cryptography, and how that explicitly describes how it utilizes them to secure the account details and how it functions.

Will be the company still marketing details regarding consumers to third parties, including advertising companies? The response, of course, should be no.

Brokers Trading Deals

Since the sorts of methods, you will rely on your objectives; the following elements should also be checked quickly to weed out investment banks that will simply not make your life easier.

Besides regular (taxable) mutual funds, what sorts of funds does a broker offer? If you already have investment income, for example, find out how you should open a health savings Arrangement (ESA) or a correctional account for the child or even other members.

Can you access a bank account? See if the broker has Roth or alternative savings plans and whether you should carry over an unused 401 K and IRA.

There are different companies for various targets for investment? For example, find out how the broker has handled accounts on offer. Often, find out which various forms of portfolios have investment requirements.

Can you use the Brokerage to manage employee retirement funds? This can apply if you are a proprietor of a business. These Account forms include Basic or SEP IRAs.

Would the fund have alternatives for Self-Directed retirement funds or the Single 401 K? What happens if you are the only team member in your small company.

3: Calculate the Charges

Although there could be some items more relevant for you other than payments, you could begin with a fairly good picture of how many you could spend to use some specific brokers.

For others, whether the product provides functionality that it lacks affordable rivals, a low prime might be acceptable. In fact, though, at valuation costs and selling profits, you ought to risk as few of the interest earned as necessary.

Beginning from the end result, you can quickly decide that stock traders have become too costly to accept and who really don't suit the sort of investing operation you're focusing on.

Brokers Account Income

Will the broker make a fee for the account opening?

Is there a Total Deposit? Please remember that investment funds have a minimum investment of $1,000 and sometimes more than that, but that isn't relevant as a financial institution that requires you to deposit the lowest possible amount of money only to open the account.

Are there really any maintenance charges per annum or yearly account? If so, were they forgiven for bigger accounts, or can they be skipped effectively even though your checking account is low? For instance, if the holders concur to collect documentation digitally, Vanguard renounces its yearly fee.

Was the dealer providing equal entry to a trade site as a result of their membership? The online platform will ideally match your needs if you are just beginning out.

There is a Pay-to-Play trading site Pro and Advanced? When you're a very seasoned user, it's crucial to learn whether or maybe not you should have to pay to update your profile or get to the speed-up software and services. For buyers who choose to position a certain amount of trades each year or spend a certain sum, certain specialized systems are safe.

What are those margin prices? Margin investing is for really professional customers only, who recognize the dangers. If you're a value player, the statement is not going to relate to you.

What is the total amount of loan and balance of the account? For greater quantities, most investment banks will give lower rates, so don't let it be a reason client borrow extra than they should.

Commissions for Trading

Will exchange commissions rely on whether you have spent or how many you move through brokerage? Vanguard's trading fees, for instance, vary according to the size of the account, whilst also E*TRADE provides a lowered council to clients who buy and sell greater than 30 times a quarter.

William Schwab's fees are smaller than rivals; however, to create an account, you will spend nearly $1,000. Think you should look at the rates that are most applicable to you, depending on your expected balance of account and trade activity.

Will common fee rates extend to information visualization? If you prepare more than stock trading, make sure that you know whatever the fees are for trading options, securities, futures, and perhaps other bonds.

If you think for investment funds or ETFs, will there be payment-free choices? What's really the least investment? Be sure that investments that allow you to purchase and sell for cheap do not charge certain forms of fees anyway. Investments often came with various types of expenses, all of which can pounce on you. Check the proposal of every investment you are contemplating to make sure you grasp all the risks involved.

Will the company, make any free or discounted transactions? The number of 'bonus' trades you earn may vary based on your outstanding balance, so be sure you double-check what's being offered for the level of your account that would apply.

Often, make sure to test what sorts of transactions apply for the reduced price — whether it's just for shares and whether it includes ETFs, futures, or specific-income securities.

Is the contract timetable favorable to the sort of trading that you can do? Are you compensated with more successful trading, or are you penalized? For example, prices for Vanguard are increasing from the first twenty-five trades for Specification and Main competitor clients, or after 100 transactions for Flagship Enable clients, as you see in the above chart. This means consumers focused on active, purchase-and-hold investments get the most value.

Conversely, for the first 30 transactions of every given fifth, E*TRADE provides discounted fees, and committed participants are paid most frequently by utilizing the site.

When the dealer offers consulting services, how many do they charge? Is there a certain balance of account required to pay for such services? When, for whatsoever the reason, you are not trying to run your own investments, make sure to pay really great consideration to advisor costs.

4: Check the Broker Network

Although every brokerage will provide a reasonably clear overview of all sorts of applications and services a trading broker provides, often giving it a quick drive is the only way to determine the consistency of the product. With brokers who require you to set up an account with free, the initiative to go through the sign-up phase might also be worthwhile only to reach the payment system if this is what's required.

If the company provides the web-based portal that can be used by anybody or a free online application needing no-string sign-up, do whatever you can to use the software that you can really need free.

Unless you're a more experienced investor, and there's no easy way to mess around in front of "Pro" software, you could get a decent understanding of a standard of the products from a brokerage only by gazing through the simple collection. Unless there is little that appears appealing in the basic model, it's doubtful that the advanced form would be value the trouble either.

But from the other side of their free services, some firms offer a vast array of gadgets and information, so just don't start writing off brokerage firms with just one platform.

We've also invested a fair deal of time shortening the options based on quality and simple account deals. Now that we have finally got to the fun part make sure to consume days reading also at features in various areas available.

Go into the steps for putting a transaction to see if the mechanism runs smoothly. Take several stock quotations and other stocks, then press on each tab to look at what sort of data the website offers. Additionally, you can search out any scanners or other resources available to help you identify funds that follow clear requirements.

Answer to the questions Whilst checking platforms:

What kinds of assets on the system may you trade? You would have already governed out any systems that do not enable you to exchange the bonds that interest you. Make sure this website helps you to transact preferred stock, IPOs, stocks, futures, and a fixed amount of income securities automatically. If you do not see clear protections on the website, but you realize it's sponsored by the company, seek to look at your settings or perform a fast check and see if you can trigger certain apps to read about authorization criteria.

Are real-time quotes? Do they flow? There are many places you could get a price estimate for just a given location, although not every one of them can have the latest up-to-date detail. Be sure you know in which you can find streaming knowledge in real-time to ensure the trades are timely. For instance, Vanguard's web-based system provides quick-time data on its countdown clock personal profiles but requires refreshing manuals. Easy results at the quote stage were postponed by 10 min more than that. Schwab's electronic quotes often entail downloading guides, but all provide real-time viewing data across the free Street-smart Edge app, and its cloud-enabled equivalent.

Can you build up your own custom watch lists or alerts? If you're trying to be a more affiliate marketer, in relation to email, you'll probably like to be able to obtain alert via text and make different watchlists various criteria.

Do the framework supply inspectors which you can personalize to discover inventories, ETFs, index funds, or any other bonds that fulfill your special requirements? Even if you're new and don't know what all of the choices literally mean, play with the different variables to have a concept of how easy to use the tools. A strong interface should be designed conceptually, and simple to use.

What sorts of commissions can you put? Go into the movements for placing the trade as well as look at what kinds of requests are being offered. A basic system should normally offer market limits, restrict, hold back, and stop boundaries. A better framework will also enable you to put chasing keep orders or consumer-on-close instructions.

If you're searching to do comparatively several transactions, and you're not concerned in a day- and swing-trading, there should be a basic choice of order types. However, if you're trying to look to get out of trading stocks gritty-gritty, you must look for just a wider choice. If you are more experienced, you will look for just the option to position contractual instructions that enable you can set up several transactions with different triggers, which will immediately execute when the requirements you define are met.

Do you really have access to the timing of orders and the implementation of trades? At least one simple platform will allow you to position good-for-day trades (meaning they could be performed at any time throughout working hours) or nice-until-canceled trades.

A more sophisticated platform allows you to position boundary orders with more variation, like put-or-kill (that cancels its order immediately if it is not filled out immediately) and Instantaneous or terminate (which cancels its order immediately if it is not filled in at least in part immediately).

Will you deal in Long Hrs.? Stock or ETF transactions arise during regular 9:30 a.m. business hours. – 16 P.M. Ap, the times of pre-market and post-hours. Each brokerage will have its own description of the different time periods covered by such extra hour's sessions. For e.g., Schwab has post-shipment trade starting at 8:00 a.m., while the before the-market sessions of E*TRADE begin around 7 a.m.

Not all systems begin trading over extra periods, and some allow only after-hours trading, not during premarket hours. You can be paid a premium for longer trading hours; just be sure that you check the conditions of certain transactions and ensure that you are not caught by surprise.

Again, that feature might not be all that good for modern investors. However, checking the extra hours trading strategy of a brokerage is important for more experienced traders or others who are trying to be very involved.

Charting Characteristics

Now that you've been messing with the application a little more take a closer look at a charting feature to test the options available for you. Listen to what sorts of data it can map, how simple it is to move among charting studies and analyzing common or industry results, and how you should modify and save to later use.

What chart patterns are on a chart? Generally, the stronger, the more. So, at the least, higher times such as quantity, RSI, exponential moving avg, swing trading, MACD, as well as stochastics, should be plottable. If one of those key guidelines is missing, it's time to move forward. Basically, a few business events, such as quarterly results, stock divides, and dividends must also be plottable.

The following are instances of two distinct technological menus. These are less than the optimal alternative. Note that volume is not plottable:

It also has an impressive technological choice, which involves several choices for each form of indicator. It also lets you map the basic data and also has a search feature:

Could you use the same map to compare various stocks or indices?

Can you draw trends, free-form graphs, Prime numbers circles, or arcs, or any other markings on the chart?

Does the website have a trade publication or any other way to save your work? If you're going to speak charts or you're a seasoned investor making notes to keep track of yourself, finding a way to design and archive your graphs is a very useful resource. Things linked include:

• Aside from building historical trends, should you easily draw on the map to illustrate key things, so you can recall when to check later?

• Can you store the maps once you have adjusted them to your needs?

• May you make information for use later?

- Would you place certain comments on the table and make sure you recognize what they refer to when you glance at them later?

Some other options

Please note that many of these choices can be accessed only on a Professional or Advanced device. If you're a successful, experienced investor, you'll definitely want to have a brokerage that provides all those options. Whether you're a more casual investor, or simply don't want to spend a fee for bells or whistles that you're not ready to, keeping to a standard free platform is perfect.

- Can you simplify trades with custom rules or with manufactured methodologies?
- Can the network be tailored to acknowledge specific price, indicator, and modulation diagram patterns?
- Can you set alerts to inform you when a contrasting pattern is found on the device?

Is the site or forum allowed to export paper? For shareholders, paper trade is a place to practice putting or performing transactions without even utilizing capital. It is a perfect place to train potential successful investors and investors with all levels of expertise to try out innovative ideas and refine their abilities without causing losses.

Is back testing enabled on the model? Back testing helps you to replicate a transaction based on the past results of your preferred defense, another method to check techniques to get familiar with the method before placing cash on a line. It's a way to put a retroactive, hypothetical transaction and then see what might have changed if you actually carried that out in actual life.

5: How well is the stockbroker teach its customers?

While a reliable and efficient payment system is important, you should take a moment to discover educational deals from the brokerage and check out another search feature.

You ought to be capable of locating for words you don't recognize or to get guidance about how to view data because you are a value player. If there is a topic you have been beginning to wonder about and a measurement you do not fully comprehend, do a test run using the search feature and see what you can efficiently find the info you really want.

Know, for one developer, what is elegant or eco-friendly can be a terrifying maze with meaningless web searches for the next, so it's essential to choose a tool that you can operate with.

If you've been navigating a site for about 20 minutes, you will be able to ask the following issues fairly quickly. If you can't, and a fast check for clear answers from the web doesn't deliver the details you need, it's usually an indication that the trading system isn't for you.

Quality and Accessibility of stockbrokers

All of the world's educational services are worthless because you can't conveniently reach them. A strong forum or website will also give a wide variety of learning resources in different formats to ensure that consumers access the content they need efficiently and conveniently in a way that fits with their preferred style. Once we delve into the different categories of educational institutions that you can anticipate from a successful brokerage, make sure that such tools were user-friendly first.

What kinds of education programs do the financial adviser offer? The layout needs to start working for you, whether it provides video clips, podcasts, podcasts, or written books.

Where does the information originate from? If the trader syndicates from other pages, guarantee all certain pages are trustworthy. If the platform features a forum or other material by readers, then please ensure that the posting writers have expertise and knowledge, which you can believe.

How easy or intuitive is navigation to the site and platform? Make sure that going to the Selling screen from a study page is a quick operation. You do not want to look like walking around in loops. Make sure the various topics on the site are easy to find.

Does a broker sell Beginners resources? This might involve pronunciation guides or how-to papers, basic analyzes, diversification of investments, how to view scientific studies and other topics for beginners.

How successful is the search feature at the platform? By typing into a common investment term or looking for subjects you have queries about, you can find this out. How quick has the search feature been able to get the details that you needed? Is this knowledge available automatically, or do you need to scroll on a few sites to get through?

Here's an instance of a non-user-friendly search function:

Although Vanguard lets you use its tracking tool to map the relative power index (RSI), its search feature does not seem to know the expression.

Resources Monitoring

Is there enough review with respect to will security? Which will provide multi-source analyst scores, real-time stories, and the market as well as sector details relevant.

Is there any of the essential data accessible? For starters, stock portfolios will contain the issuance company's historical records, such as annual releases, financial results (like working capital, operating statement and statement of cash), dividend distributions, trading volume and repurchases, and SEC disclosures. Any insider-trading operation must also be warned.

Are business details open for US and global markets? How regarding information from manufacturing and from the sector? How thoroughly can you immerse yourself in the big picture circumstances affecting business performance?

6: Ease of Depositing and Withdrawing Funds

Is there enough review with respect to will security? Which will provide multi-source analyst scores, real-time stories, and the market as well as sector details relevant.

Is there any of the essential data accessible? For starters, stock portfolios will contain the issuance company's historical records, such as annual releases, financial results (like working capital, operating statement and statement of cash), dividend distributions, trading volume and repurchases, and SEC disclosures. Any insider-trading operation must also be warned.

Are business details open for US and global markets? How regarding information from manufacturing and from the sector? How thoroughly can you immerse yourself in the big picture circumstances affecting business performance?

Removing Funds

How long would it take to recover the funds from selling the investments? Making sure you test the unified group with the numerous forms of shares that you are trying to sell.

What are income payments or tax payments? How quick are those assets available to invest? For retiring?

How convenient is using the investment account to remove funds? Figure out how you can transfer through ACH wire, wire, or email and also how far it would take to get into your banking account for all those funds. Test to figure out whether there is a withdrawal charge, too.

Will the broker offer the option of adding a debit and ATM card to your credit card? It is often given for a mutual fund, as well as other times to use this service; you have to open a connected checking and saving account. Find out what other ATMs you can use if you have a card option, so there are some costs involved with using the card.

7: Support to Customers

By now, you've already limited your choices to one of two brokerage firms that actually blow you up in terms of money, functionality, and functionality. If you've reached the dream forum, or are already on the board, just take a couple more minutes to search a brokerage aid section, you're contemplating.

When you're a potential user and feel stressed, make absolutely sure you can rapidly and effectively get in contact with the military members. When you're technologically inept, try to ensure your tech support department is easy to get in contact with and accessible 24/7.

Although these things won't make and break a brokerage choice, it's always important to know you recognize where and where to get support.

- Is there a designated amount where you should call a person asking for trade aid?
- Ensure you are informed of any potential phone-assisted trading costs.
- Can you call an automatic number for the simple queries?
- Ultimate support what? And what were the Assistance ask-in hours?

- What are the operating hours for telephone lines? Will you dial 24/7, or is it the phones working outside office hours only?
- There is an email for those that are opposed to contacting that you use to get timely support?
- Does the company use a safe network for internal transmission of relevant documentation and client questions?
- Does the blog have an immediate online support option?
- Maybe you are having a normal issue but don't want to annoy the member? Is there a viewable FAQ segment that responds to a large range of perspectives?
- How for tech backing? Are there specific phone lines, telephone numbers, or chat networks to access professional support?

8: Go and take Next Moves

Whatever broker has by far the most active campaign, we realize it can be enticing to sign up for. However, good investing takes dedication to details far before you position your first order.

If you're planning to take trading a lengthy-term hobby, a long-term career, or even a way to boost your pension fund, then it's important to use the resources and tools that will help you deal for an enjoyable and successful experience.

Hopefully, by adopting it an in-depth tutorial, you've found the forum that would better fit your requirements, which they may be. On our stockbroker rating page, you will find support filtering via the various brokers.

Chapter 8: capital saving and rules for option trading

We'll discuss index alternatives in this segment, and how it could be included as parts of your total trading strategy. And we go on to give a few other recommendations as to how to approach stock trading initially. Different optional forms are used daily. For the house and vehicle, you have protection to cover the home against an unexpected disaster on which you are charged a nominal fee called a premium. In the same manner, creditors will buy strategy research as equity protection.

Capital retention may be each bit as critical to the long-term return on investment as price appreciation. Yeah, any investor will expect steady improvements all the way, but occurrences outside the control will trigger a brief decrease in your stock value. Preferred shares help you to minimize the danger of particular positions, and market indices enable you to shield the investment as a whole and against unexpected events.

8.1 Index Options — A valuable investment manager tool

Index rights rates are focused on a wide market sample, instead of on a specific portfolio. Dividends offer you the opportunity to purchase or sell a Hundred shares of a common company. Even so, you cannot include dual shares in hundreds in securities with market index, because "exercising" just involves having the gap in cash here between market valuation and the fair value. But much of the similar terminology, methods, and principles that we've been learning extend equally well to these tools.

The idea of market index started in 83 because when the Chicago board of options Market (CBOE) started selling options on a 100-stock index. It was named the Exchange Options Index and has been shortened as OEX. Today, this measure usually exchanges more than $20 million worth of contracts per day and is also in the top fifty among the most popular options. The Dow Jones Manufacturing Indexes (DJX), an S&P 499 (SPX), the Cincinnati Automatics-Conductor Indexes (SOX), a NASDAQ Hundred (NDX), and hundreds of other indexes related to a specific business or sector are also accessible.

Index futures may be utilized to bet about certain stocks' potential price changes, and many of the exact approaches we've been working through for equity futures will be added. Even so, here we would concentrate on using strategy research to protect, or hedge, an investment against a large downturn in the sector while in the meantime encouraging the portfolio to take part in any sector advance.

The main clients for indexes products are banks and investment funds. They manage huge, diverse nest eggs, and buying puts over a measurement or sector is simpler on them than buying them on dozens of single stocks. When they consider whether to mitigate their danger, they have to weigh the strategy's expense with their customer perception. Index starts to put really aren't cheap, so why would these managers risk underachieve the industry by 3 percent over a nine-month period (around a 13.2 percent annual rate)? The boss is

Prepared to accept the chance whether he or she has a bullish outlook, and expecting to win the price by taking advantage of puts. The index buying option aims to restrict or protect against fundamental concern.

Uncertainty is a significant risk factor, and index contracts have greater volatility than actual equity options. When you exchange an index choice, your income or loss is not related to a single market price. The index 's aggregate composition defines its worth, so it has a masking impact on price shifts.

The "avg" impact on market index implies that for certain element stock options, they appear to sell in a generally smaller range than average. Another aspect that allows index options less risky is that they're not as likely to be at risk as firms. A single event like a merger or a suddenly low-income report will not impact the measurement as much as the personal stock does. Just as a bond fund utilizes a broad equity pool to produce a more stable return, the index often gains from the same consolidating impact compared to its constituent stocks.

8.2 Use Index Options to securing your portfolio

The fund hedging strategy is clear. Find the benchmark with the structure that most perfectly aligns your own account, and then buy security puts that are out of pocket. Unlike share options, when you realize you intend to buy one put for each and every 100 equity shares you hold, it's impossible that the fund would contain exactly that same shares as the benchmark, and not precisely the very same ratio. Measures such as investment delta allow investors to come near, but trying to hedge an actual investment is a little art. Your target is the uncommon part of a strategy: purchase takes, but instead, hope that they will expire unused!

A fund manager, odd as it may seem, simply expects the without-money putting options would expire pointlessly. After all, an upright homeowner is not expecting his house will be burned down, and insurance coverage can payback. Likewise, a stock manager who purchases in out-of-the-money sells is not expecting that the economy will fall and that his fund will lose value by lesser than the total price. It is a hard-to-understand term for other creditors. But a skilled fund manager acknowledges that there are occasions whenever a sharp price correction, whilst not predicted, has a strong enough likelihood of happening to rationalize the out:

of-the-money expenditure of 1 percent to 3 percent of the holdings puts of 1 to 3 weeks of health care.

You could also use strategy research to ensure, to some degree, other positions. For instance, if you've spent part in your holdings in stocks of the managed fund, you might be able to purchase index choice puts to safeguard your stocks in the incident of a general value downturn. It means that (1) the benchmark you pick computes the mutual fund's stock assets and (2) you think the market is going upward, yet you accept the risk what your timing will be wrong. The match may not be accurate, but the approach has one purpose: to predict and defend against widespread decreases of a type that we all have seen in recent times. Markets tend to move usually in the very same path, so when the total market does, stocks – even those whose individual dynamics are strong – decline. By the same logic, at minimum to some degree, a solid bull market continues to drive most shares in an increasing direction, even underperformers.

8.3 Use Index Options for Diversification and Speculation

Index methods may be used to guess, too. Here those who offer the long-term growth advantage, which helps you avoid an all too classic error of merely selecting the opposite stock. Your choice may be well placed, but you might choose the incorrect equity. So, whereas a sector could perform heavily as a community, it's one exception is a stock you're investing all of your capital in! Consolidation has also been a major attraction for investors by mutual funds;

And this functions as well for buyers or investors of options. Many people believe its enough liquidity to buy shares in five separate stocks, but in a depressed economy, all five may collapse in value. Many people believe purchasing stock in mutual funds is a smart option. Mutual funds also have a range of disadvantages:

1. Control bills at tax. An annual fee is charged by each mutual fund, a proportion of the investment that goes to the management salaries. If share prices increase or fall, this cost is chargeable. You charge a trading charge to both sides of the market index, but otherwise, you retain all the money.

2. A Lot might contribute, too. Many equity funds, as many as eight percent of all the money you spend, are often subjected to a loading tax. So, you only have $92 at work for each and every $hundred dollars you're bringing money. The charging fee refunds your expenditure, even if the fund is doing poorly. Why earn a commission on sales? If you are smart enough just to explore alternatives, you should not use a dealer from a managed fund to tell about how to invest your money. When you need to participate in a fund, choose a hardly any-load; they've done traditionally on a level with the loaded funds, so you don't need to help a salesman as much as placing your money at risk.

3. Without liquidity, you still put money at risk. When people purchase the stock of investment funds, you buy at a level of 100 percent, without any leverage. That means your whole portfolio is at the maximum price, at risk. And if the fund's valuation slips, then you've wasted it. In recent times, millions of creditors have been found to be investing in investments whose actual market valuation is well below the interest they spend. Whether they take a loss, or they stay closely hoping for the economy to change around — only to get toward their homes. This issue is eliminated for index options since the only vulnerability (at least in futures contracts) is the cost of the amount paid, which is a percentage of the index prices that you manage.

4. Diversifying of wealth may be going toward you. One of Wall Street's "dirty secrets" is liquidity isn't always a

financially viable calculated decision. If the actual quality of the market is poor, so a good-diversified investment is sure to damage value. Diversification gives some relief for an individual who doesn't grasp how the economy works. Just a limited number of all stock funds did ultimately exceed the average index, though. In general, the amazing long-term yields claimed in brochures from mutual funds are the consequence of reinvested investment income, not just because a fund has some insight on which shares to buy.

As a rule of thumb, stakeholders tend to think about upward price action in terms of timing. One would prefer to purchase cheap and sell big. But if you're using individual company stock or market indices, don't overstate the put. If the downward trend in the market is, you can earn as much capital, or more, purchasing puts as you want to when you purchase calls in anticipation of a turnaround of price change. Most shareholders seem to be untreatable realists and begin to assume of puts for only health coverage or as a portion of other profit-making strategies when prices are rising.

Chapter 9: Common mistakes to avoid and suggestions

If stocks move up, down, and sideways it is possible to benefit by selling options. With a fairly tiny cash outlay, you might use option methods to sell stocks, preserve gains and control huge parts of the stock.

Sounds nice, doesn't it? Here we have the pick.

You may also risk more by buying options than the overall sum you've spent over a fairly short span of time. That is why continuing with caution is so necessary. Also, self-confident investors will misjudge a chance and lose capital.

It addresses the top 10 errors that novice options traders usually make, with professional advice from our in-house advisor, Brian Gitomer, about how you might trade wiser. Take time now to study them, so you can prevent an expensive wrong move.

Misaligned Leverage

Many rookies abuse contracts providing leveraging factor alternatives, without knowing how much chance they are taking. They 're also attracted to making quick-term calls. So, this is so often the case, it's important to ask: Is it a "speculative" or "conservative" strategy to buy outright calls?

Leverage of a Master. A general rule to start option investors: if you're usually trading 100 stock lots, then stay with one start option. When you usually exchange 300 lots of securities- maybe 3 agreements. That is a decent volume of training to start with. When you don't have luck in small scales, the bigger scale trades would more definitely not be successful.

Not being responsive to new initiatives.

Most option traders claim they 'd never purchase out: of-the-money stocks or offer the options in-the-money. Such absolutes sound stupid — till after you find oneself in a market that is working against you.

There have also been experienced options for investors. Confronted by this situation, you are sometimes inclined to violate all kinds of ethical rules.

You have also learned, as a bond investor, a common excuse for scaling up to keep up. For e.g., if you loved the stock when you purchased it at 80, at 50, you have to love it. It may be enticing to purchase more on the exchange to reduce the total cost level. Be vigilant though: In the field of options, what provides a sense for shares does not float. Typically boosting up as a potential tactic just doesn't make any sense.

Be accessible to exploring different approaches to invest in futures. Note, options are securities, implying that their values don't shift the same or have almost the same characteristics as the stock market. A decline in time, whether positive or poor, for the role, must also be taken into account in the strategies.

When things will change in your business, and you contemplate what was previously inconceivable, just honestly ask yourself: was this a move I took when I first started opening this status?

If the reaction is no, so do not.

Close a trade, cut down on your damages, or start a different chance that makes perfect sense today. Options give decent leverage opportunities on comparatively low assets, but when you dig deeper, they can explode just as rapidly as every position. Take a minor risk because it presents you with an opportunity to eventually escape a disaster.

Wait Much long to Order Limited Options.

This failure can be distilled down with one word of wisdom: Always be eager and able to buy out shorter options soon.

Too many traders may take too long to purchase back their sold options. There are many million explanations for doing this. For instance:

- You don't want the tribunal to the bill.
- You're hoping that the deal ends void.
- You're only looking to get a bit more from the exchange.

Just when to give the short options back. If OTM gets lost with your short alternative and you can purchase it back to profitably take the danger off the table, do it. Don't be greedy about that.

For example, what if you offered a choice for $1.00, and now it's worth 20 percent? To start with, you wouldn't offer a 20: cent option, as it would just not be worth it. Equally, you must not believe scraping out the remaining few cents from this deal is worth it.

Here's a simple thumb rule: if you may keep 80 percent or more of the original income from the choice deal, you can definitely buy it back. This is a virtual guarantee, otherwise. A few of these weeks, you'll bite back by a short choice because you took too long.

Putting in spreads

Many traders with starting options seek to "pull-in" a gap by first purchasing the choice and then selling a second choice. They seek to cut the amount by a handful of pennies. That's just not worth the chance.

Comfortable sound? That example, too, has fried most seasoned options traders and taught the valuable lesson.

When you decide to swap a set, don't "jump in" Deal one set as a one-time deal. Don't needlessly take on excessive business pressure.

You could purchase a call, for instance, and then seek to schedule the selling of some other call, trying to get out of the second leg a little bit better. If the economy experiences a fall, this is a risky tactic, because they won't be capable of carrying off the profit. You may be faced with a call option, with little plan to move on.

If you're trying the whole strategic plan, don't buy the spread but also wait approximately, hoping the economy will be moving in the favor. You may imagine you might market it at a better price later. This is a rather unlikely performance.

Also, view a split as one deal. Don't want to solve the pacing minutia. Before the economy keeps going down, you should get into a trade.

Ignoring the Stocks for Fair Markets Table

Person inventories may be very unpredictable. For instance, if a company has a large unpredicted news event, this could rock a stock for a couple of days. On the other side, even extreme chaos in a large company that is a member of an S&P 500 will certainly not trigger the index would fluctuate significantly.

What are the story's morals?

Options trading focused on benchmarks will protect your part from the tremendous changes that individual news reports may produce for selected securities. Take into account neutral transactions on big indicators, and reduce the unsure impact of news from the market.

Find investment tactics that may be lucrative if the sector already sits on indices, including a short break (also named margin requirements). Index moves appear to be much less intense than some other methods, and far less likely to be impacted by media.

Traditionally, the short spread is built for income, even though the fundamental value stays the same. Short position spreads are thus deemed "fair to bearish," and short puts spread are "good to bullish." This is one of the main distinctions between longer spreads or short spread.

Note, spreads include trading in greater than one alternative, and thus incur and over one fee. Hold that in factors when choosing the choices on trade.

Not realizing what to do at the task

If you offer options, just periodically inform yourself that you may be allocated early, until the expiry date. Most new retail investors never dream about assigning as a prospect before such time that it occurs. When you haven't factored into the assignment, it can be confusing, particularly if you are operating a multi-leg approach like short or long spreads.

For instance, what if you run a call option spread and are given the short higher-strike option? Starting traders may panic or exercise the long option to utilize the stock for the lower hit. This is definitely not the right choice, though. Selling the long choice on the stock market, taking the residual time premium together with the intrinsic interest of the contract, and utilizing the profits to purchase the order, is typically cheaper. Then at a higher price, you will buy the company to the individual investor.

An early appointment is one of the often-unpredictable market activities which are genuinely emotional. When it occurs, there is always no rhyme or explanation behind it. It is all true. And as the economy shows, it's a trick less than genius.

If delegated well in advance, go about what you will do. The greatest defense towards the early task is to let it play into your early thought. Otherwise, it will lead you to make less than rational, in-the-moment, protective decisions.

Taking consumer dynamics into account will aid. -- one is more prudent to work out early, for example? A call or a put? Trying to exercise a put or stock sale right ensures the dealer sells the stock or gets cash.

Always question oneself: Do you like your money now or when it expires? Citizens often prefer cash now or cash later on. This implies the puts appear to be more prone to earlier activity than calls.

A calling implies that the dealer must be able to invest cash to buy the product, relative to the game later. Waiting for and investing the cash later is typically human nature. When an inventory is rising, though, less qualified traders can squeeze the pin early, lacking to know that they are leaving a certain time premium mostly on table. How will an early task be random?

Failure of Reality for Next Event

Not all market developments are predetermined. However, there are two important things to keep on top of while selling options- profits and dates of dividends on the stock market.

For starters, if you've sold puts and a payout is coming, it improves the chances that you may be allocated early because the choice is already in cash. This is particularly true if we consider the dividend to be increasing. That's the proprietors of options that have no dividend protection. Options traders will exercise the right to receive, and by the common assets.

Make sure things weigh pending. You'll need to learn the former-dividend date, for starters. Stay well clear of offering put options with unpaid distributions, unless you are able to consider higher assignment costs.

Trading with the company's securities during the price action normally ensures that you may face greater uncertainty - and therefore pay an elevated cost for that opportunity. If you intend to buy a choice during the profit-taking, then one choice is to buy another option and offer another, producing a spread.

Illiquid options trading

Cash flow is about how fast a trader could even buy this without causing major movement in price. A smart investor is one that often contains available, committed sellers and buyers.

Here's a way to talk about everything: Liquidity relates to the possibility the next transaction can be carried over at a rate equivalent to the previous.

Options markets are, for one basic explanation, more competitive to option markets. Investment bankers swap only one stock, while rational investors can select from hundreds of strike prices.

For instance, investment bankers would rush to one type of let's just assume, IBM stock; however, brokerage firms may have six separate expirations to choose from a host of strike rates. By nature, further choices imply that the price action would generally not be as competitive as the equity market.

A good reason like IBM is not normally a liquidity issue for stock traders and options traders. Narrower inventories creep into the issue. Take extreme Green Technologies, an environmentally sustainable (imaginary) energy business of some hope, can have only one stock that sells once per week by request.

The stocks on extreme Green Technologies are likely to be much more negative if the portfolio was illiquid. Typically, this will allow the gap between the offer and leading to a "to have the options excessively high.

For e.g., whether the bid-ask difference is $0.20, then if you purchase the contract $2.00, that's a maximum of 10 percent of a price charged to determine the place.

It's never a smart decision to place your role right away at a 10 percent loss, even by picking a highly leveraged alternative with a broad bid-ask range.

Trading overleveraged options push up the expense of doing so, and on a yearly basis, price action prices are now greater than stocks. Don't place yourselves on a load.

If selling stocks, please ensure that the available position is at least 40 times the size of the connections that you choose to sell.

For e.g., to exchange a 10-lot, the appropriate leverage must be 10 x 40, or perhaps a minimum of 400 open interest. Open value reflects the number of option contracts left with a market price and expiry date that were bought or exchanged to put it up. Any closing payments raise the open value, although it reduces the closure of payments. Also, at the end of each financial day is measured the free interest. Invest liquidity options to avoid extra expenses and pressures on yourself. There are tons of possibilities somewhere for liquids.

Search for resources that can assist you in discovering possibilities, obtain perspective, or respond when the urge attacks? Find out our Trade platform's smart devices.

Doesn't have an escape route

You have always seen it before, a thousand times. It's important to manage the emotions when bulk purchases, much like stocks. That does not involve swallowing all the worries in a human - level way. It's far better than all that: Get a job schedule and adhere to it.

You have to have an escape schedule, time frame. Except though things fall your side. Use an upside-out stage, a downward escape stage, and well-advanced timescales for each departure.

What if you head out though early and drop it upside hand on the ground?

That is the preoccupation of a traditional dealer. Here's the perfect counterpoint: what about if you reliably made a profit, then the frequency of injuries, and sleep well at night?

Establish a strategy for the exit. Whether you purchase or sell shares, an escape strategy is an utter necessity. This lets you develop more efficient trading patterns. This, therefore, maintains some power over the fears.

Evaluate an upside-down escape strategy but the worst-case situation you 're able to accept. If you accomplish your objectives on the upside, transparent your place, and take all your money. Don't feel gloat. If you hit your stop-loss downside, you can clear your place once again. Don't subject yourself to unnecessary danger by betting that the price of the right can return.

Perhaps from start to end, the urge to break this guidance will be high. Use so not. You have to build a decision, but instead commit to it. All too many merchants draw out a schedule and then throw the strategy to suit their impulses as long as the exchange is done.

Call Options for (OTM)

Buying OTM strikes openly is some of the most challenging ways to reliably earn money in options trading. Margin requirement sell options cater to traders of fresh options since they are inexpensive.

Begin would seem like a reasonable place: Purchase the best escorts alternative and see whether you can select a winner. Calls to purchase should sound comfortable as it fits the trend you 're used to pursuing as a stock trader: trade away and seek and sell big. Yet if you restrict yourself to that technique alone, you will continually lose capital.

Try offering an OTM long position on an already held portfolio as the first approach. This method is regarded as a strategic concealed call.

What's good with protected calls as a tactic is that if the call is secured by a cash position, the danger will not arise from buying the right. This even has the ability to give you market profits while you're optimistic but also able to sell the shares if the price goes up. This tactic will give you the "look" of how contract rates for the OTM option shift when the approaches to expiry and the changes in market demand.

Nonetheless, the danger resides in controlling a stock – as well as the danger may be big. Although offering the covered call does not create capital danger, it does reduce the upside, thereby increasing the possibility of opportunity. If the price increases and your request is executed, you face needing to buy the shares after the assignment.

Need to build your own trading strategy for options? Check through our newcomers, seasoned, and professionals' segment for free.

Chapter 10: Leaps strategy to win the great reward

If you are optimistic about the stock of a specific firm, you can arrange your portfolio of longer-term equity expectation bonds (LEAPS). A 50 percent increase might turn into a 300 percent benefit, but this approach carries risks, as well as the odds against you, are stacked. It will scrub out the whole investment in a couple of days while it is foolishly being used.

Using carefully, though, this can be a valuable device helping you to maximize the returns on investment without raising funds on the margin.

What LEAPS actually Are?

LEAPS is a lengthy-term equity trading option for an expiry date of the above 3 years.1 Purchasing such options helps you to just use fewer money than you've bought shares, so they will produce enormous gains if they invest correctly in the context of the stocks.

Buy explicitly or on Margins.

For the $14,500, you could actually purchase 1,000 stock shares directly, or you might convert 2 to 1 by investing in interest, taking the overall contribution around $29,000 or 2,000 stock shares with a $14,500 partially offset loan.

But if you have a margin offer, the stock drops, and they can't get funds from some other lender to invest in your bank, you might be compelled to sell assets.

You'll now have to make payments on the benefit of slightly lending the capital.

LEAPS over Actually Buy Stock

Let's imagine you choose to buy some Business XYZ stock. It's $14.50 selling, so you've got $14,500 for spending. You are persuaded that within 12 months or 2, XYZ would be significantly higher because you have to spend your capital in the inventory. You need 3 choices. You may buy the goods straight away, purchase it moderately, or using LEAPS.

Profit purchasing means lending funds from the broker to use it and offering the stock as loan leverage. It sounds nice, but eventually, you may risk more cash than you have spent.

How LEAPS Could Work

There are a few more different directions this situation will turn out.

- If the option sells around $17.51 or $19 each share before the choice ends in 2 years, you will incur a capital loss of 100 percent if it falls below the $17.50 option market price.

- If the market rises significantly, you may call the brokerage and close your spot.

- You could compel somebody to offer the stock to you at $17.50 a share and instead turn back quickly and offer the securities you purchased at a lower current share price if you want to use your rights. You'd be pocketing $6 a share — the $7.50 taxable income less the $1.50 that you charged for both the option — if it increased to $100.

That investing strategy really sounds like you're saying the stock is worth significantly as much as the market price — maybe $10 to $15 more — before the shares expire.

Utilizing LEAPS

Unless you don't really like this amount of exposure, you may suggest utilizing LEAPS rather than the popular stock. Next, look at the trading tables released by a Toronto stock exchange Market (Cboe) to note how you can buy a Business XYZ call choice with a discount rate at $17.50.4, which expires 2 years within the next.

A call approach provides you a given time span within which you may acquire securities at the purchase price.5

This ensures you get the option to buy a share at $17.50 at any point between the date of acquisition and the date of expiration. For this alternative, you have to pay a charge or premium. The pay was mostly offered in 100-share contracts each.

Let's presume you're going to take the $14,500 to acquire 100 deals. Recall for any deal includes 100 securities, and you're now entitled to 10,000 Business XYZ securities with the LEAPS. Let's presume you've charged a $1.50 bonus per unit. That is indeed $1.50 x 10,000, or $15,000 worth.

You have rounded up the investment target to the closest appropriate number because the stock is actually priced at $14.50 a share. You had the option to purchase it at $17.50 a quarter, and with that privilege, you pay $1.50 a share, and the breakeven is $19 a share.

The Value of Utilizing LEAPS

For allocation of just $1.50 each share, the overall income on the deal will be $6 each share. By utilizing LEAPS alone, you converted a 72.4 percent rise in market price into such a 400 percent boost. Your vulnerability has definitely risen; however, despite the opportunity for enormous returns, you have been paid for that.

Your gains equate to $1 million with just $6000 in initial expenditure. This is similar to a $10,500 you'd receive if you buy outright 500 shares of a company at an appraised value around $14.50, so it rose with time to $25 a share.

Buying it at a discount would have let you raise $21,000, so you'd have minimized the possibility of wipe-out as something over the $14.50 buying price would've been a benefit. During your ownership time, you might have earned dividend payments, but you'd have needed to pay tax on the spread you lent from your dealer.

It's quite likely that if the economy tanked, you might have been immune to the liquidity event.

The LEAPS Risks and Temptations

To most creditors, use LEAPS does not really make sense. We can be used only with extreme care, for all who:

• Experience strategic commercialization

• Have enough of overspending cash

• Can manage to risk any penny it puts on the market

• Have a full portfolio which won't lose the losses caused by an active strategy of this sort.

The greatest challenge in utilizing LEAPS is just to transform some potentially successful trading choices into a high-risk bet by picking shares that have poor pricing, or it will require a complete miracle to meet the market price.

You may also be persuaded by taking less costly, smaller-duration alternatives which are no longer deemed Jumps, to take on even more time risk. The incentive is exacerbated by the exceedingly uncommon occasions in which an investor has produced an absolute fortune.

The Bridge does not include policy, fee, savings, or financial resources. The details will be viewed without regard to any individual investor's investment interests, risk appetite, or monetary circumstances and may not be ideal for investors. Past success doesn't suggest potential outcomes. Investing entails threats of future principal damages.

Chapter 11: Low and high volatility trading environments

Options trading is much more than bullish and bearish, or neutral to the market. There is volatility in there. Cost restrictions. The dimensional biases are weaker or stronger. Whatever the case, you have to pick a rational choice approach that can be threat-defined, money-effective and/or have a better chance of benefit than either purchasing or short selling stock.

You will construct a helpful reference guide by grouping through technique into buckets containing through possible mixture of those three factors. You might also print this out and wall-tape it. Doing so may help you go through a process of creating quick investment decision if you need them or if they are warranted.

With this set of tactics tailored for an increased-volatility economic environment we can help you get going. Note how much of the simple vertical & calendar spread are made of. When you study them, bear in mind that such approaches do not provide any assurances. A surge in volatility is a result of enhanced instability and, generally, market fluctuation.

High vol typically means higher prices for options that you may try and take benefit of with simple premium methods. High vol makes you find additionally (OTM) out: of-the-money option deals that can deliver large chances of expiring useless and theoretically better returns on cash. Pushing further short OTM options also means techniques have more space for all the share price to move in opposite direction, because they lose revenue. Here are some few bearish, bullish, and impartial methods designed to scenarios of high volatility.

11.1 Increased volatility

Quick OTM put the bullish plan

Framework: Sell a put, purchase lesser-strike placed at the same expiration date.

Working Capital: lower; relies on strike differences.

RISK: Set.

Traders recommend utilizing this technique when the short-put capital demand becomes too big after a portfolio, or when chosen by established risk. Traders may be seeking compensation for a small vertical about 1/3 of the strike diameter. Commonly, analytical tools expiring in the simple premium "sweet spot," again, generally approximately 20–40 days in. Some traders build a limited OTM puts vertically by searching for OTM put, which has high likelihood (maybe 65-70 percent) of a set to expire uselessly, then aim at purchasing additional OTM put into trying and getting the desired credit, usually between one and two more OTM hits.

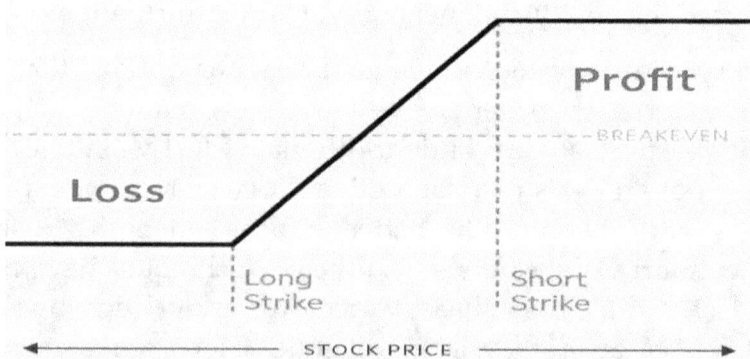

Short Exposed Put – bullish plan

Framework: Sell put

CAPITAL need: higher

RISK: Logically established, it may go all of the ways to zero as a stock, but no lower. So, zero could be a long journey while it's defined.

Someone with an investment in this strategy may suggest considering for OTM shares that are highly likely to expire worthless and good return on investment. Underwriting standards for high-priced equities are higher; the low-priced stocks are lower. The size of an account can determines whether or not you could make the trade. Many buyers, based on the degree of implied uncertainty, future events, or business releases, may search for the termination in the small premium "sweet spot," usually around 20 and 40 days out. Pointing the balance spot is aimed at balancing growing positive decay time even with-high increased wealth. If the share price drops, as well as short placed, is assigned, choose a stock that you're pleasant owning. You will want to find a covered call option towards your long stock stake if this occurs.

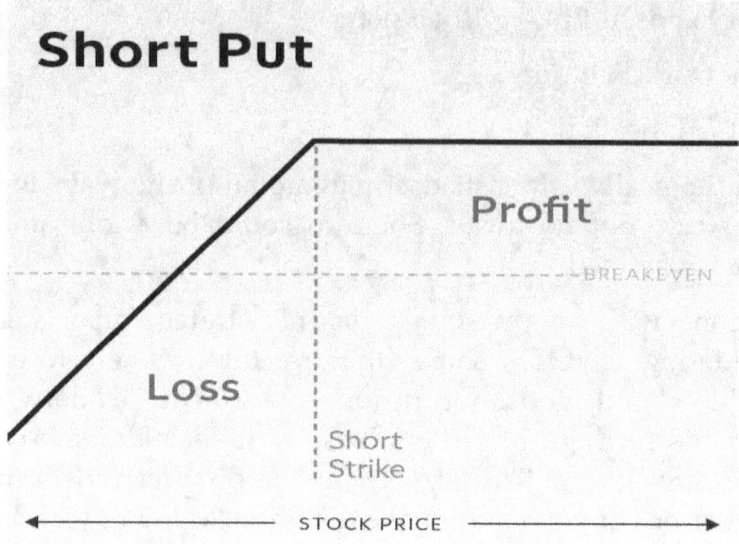

Long butterfly-bearish plan for an unstable call.

Framework: 1 call buy, 3 higher-strike calls sell, 2 higher-strike calls buy; equidistant strikes.

Need of capital: lower; depends on long and short strikes.

RISK: Specified.

A combination of a vertical OTM call and long at-the-money (ATM) call butterfly or marginally OTM call. This should have been a credit spread, where the butterfly debt is offset by the credit from the short vertical. That is not strongly bearish because if stock is in a short strike of an integrated butterfly, the full benefit is gained. Even if an unbalanced sell butterfly is launched for a profit if the stock declines and the options in the place expire worthlessly, it will not lose value.

NOTE: It can be difficult to find strike combinations that require you to activate a credit when vol is especially large. You might need to conduct some extra work to identify applicants who will offer you a discount upfront. If your preference is bullish instead of a bearish outlook, you might find an unbalanced put-butterfly consisting of the same ratio of 1-3-2, operating just down from the ATM and in equidistant attacks. Several traders consider an unstable put butterfly for a credit harder to start.

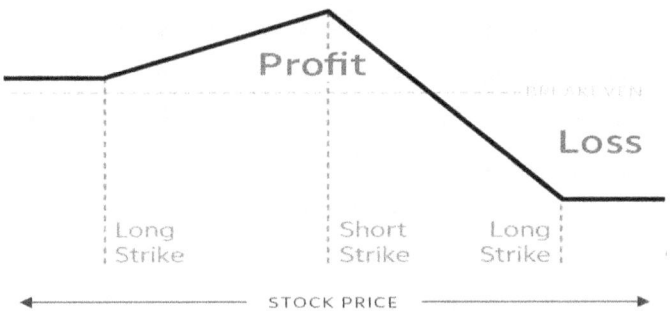

Long Unbalanced Call Butterfly

Bearish strategic planning No. 1: Vertical Call for short OTM

Framework: Sell call, purchase greater-strike call with the same expiry.

CAPITAL Criteria: Smaller, but the gap between the strikes depends

Danger: Defined

Any traders tend to set the exchange credit at 30 percent of the strikes gap. Start searching at the "sweet spot" for exhaustion, usually from 20 and 50 days away. Build by searching for the OTM call, which has a strong chance of set to expire meaningless (again, maybe 65-70 percent), then check at purchasing another OTM call and try and get the desired credit, usually between one and two more OTM hits.

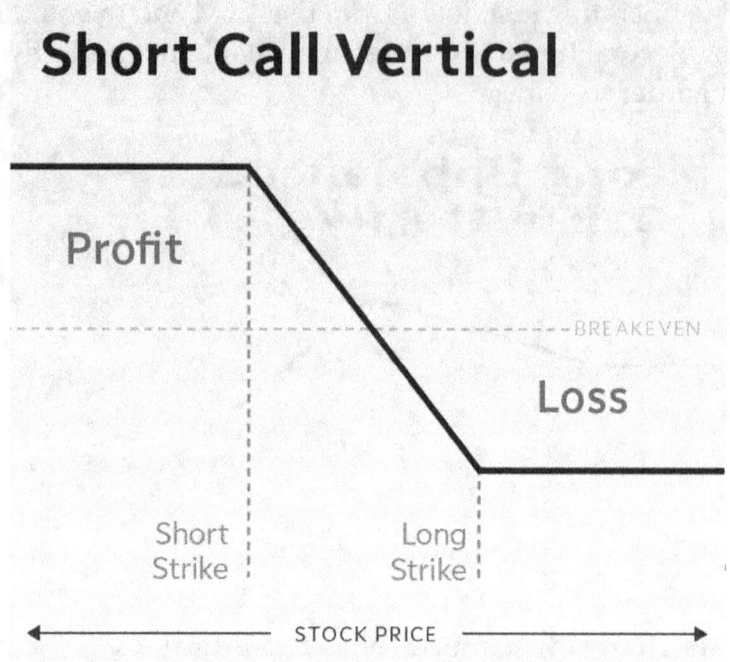

Long request or call for a butterfly- building strategy 1

Framework: Purchase 1 option with a lower strike, offer two options with a higher strike, buy 1 option with a higher strike, both calls or puts, both strikes exactly halfway.

CAPITAL Necessity: Inferior

Danger: Defined.

A maximum benefit is gained while the stock would be at the expiry of a short middle hit. Traders can put a slightly OTM short mid-strike to get minor bias in direction. Because of a large butterfly 's small benefit spectrum, the chance of income is typically less than 50 percent. High uncertainty holds ATM butterflies smaller in value. Butterflies are growing in value as expiration progresses more quickly, and buyers can look for options that expire within 14 working days. Simple gamma increases significantly at expiry when the inventory is at a short strike. Consider taking revenue — if available — before expiration to stop turning butterflies with a last-second price swing into a loser.

NOTE: Butterflies are low-risk but reward big. Often, they're cheap to initiate. For a cause, some traders would claim they're cheap, which is because optimizing a butterfly's return needs not only a precise target throughout the share price but also precision timing.

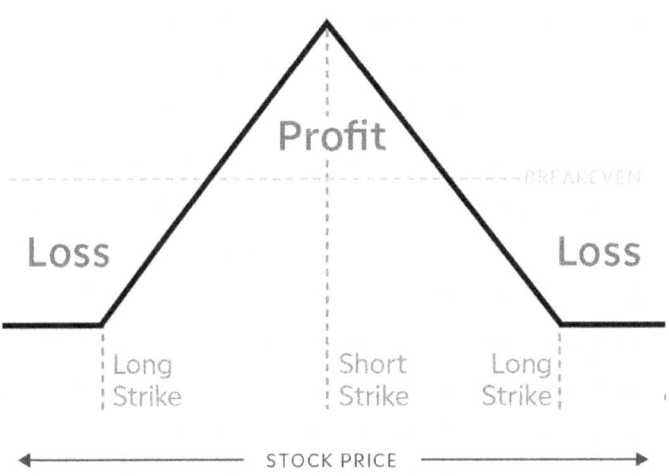

Iron Condor-Policy enormous strategy 2:

Framework: sell vertical lower-strike, offer vertical greater-strike call, span from long to short hits.

Working Capital: lower; based on strike difference

Suggest applying the compensation to a set amount of exchange, such as 40 percent of the gap between shorter and longer hits (e.g., $0.80 or greater of the iron condor of $2 of size). Traders usually try termination in what considered to be the "sweet spot" short premium, traditionally between 5 and 40 days away, to match the key positive decay yet with-great extrinsic interest. Higher volume lets anyone find additional OTM calls or puts that are extremely likely to expire uselessly but with a large premium. Investors may build the iron condor through buying additional OTM choices, normally a strike or two. You may not want to place it on for credit so low doesn't matter how big the likelihood, because incentives on four legs will often eat up much of the possible income.

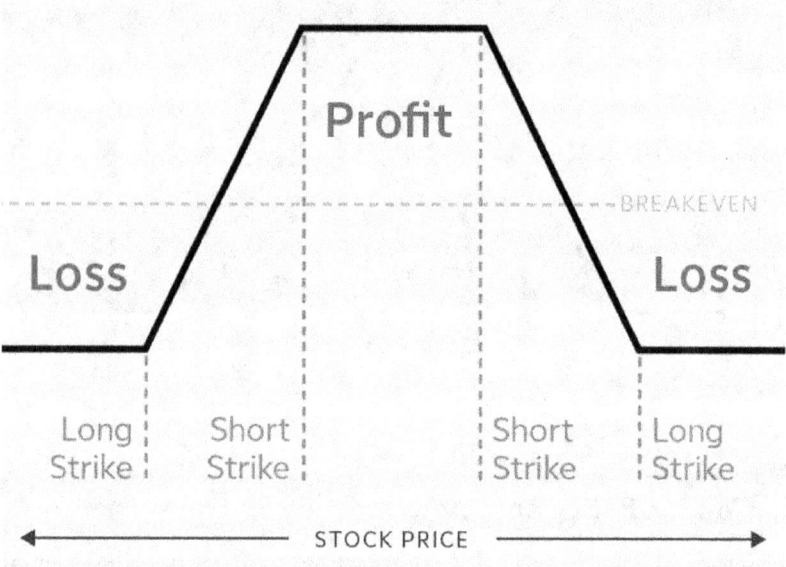

11.2 High Turnover Profits

The absence of uncertainty on the share market in 2017 has recently changed headlines, only with S&p 500 experiencing a smooth, steady ride to new highs. In reality, despite the Brexit crisis, the last moment the SPX fell 3 percent or more is June 24, 2015. Against this context, we agreed to dissolve the four-legged stocks method that will enable you to leverage on time of subdued, close to zero-volatility market action during a stock market: an iron condor.

What is actually an Iron Condor?

An iron condor is basically the mix of quick call spread or short put split, and — as in any of those techniques — the overall possible benefit is confined to an original net credit. Conversely, one may speak of an iron condor as a more traditional variant of the quick strangle.

The twin sold options also at inner shares form the condor's "ass," and two bought options at the external strikes reflect the "wings." An intention of the investor is to hold the common assets at the dual sold strikes by expiry options, where this case all four options may be left to expiration worthlessly.

Example of an iron condor.

Stock XYZ has given the last couple of weeks varying from $25 to $27. You foresee this directional channel to stay steady in the near term, particularly with the upcoming profits releasing a huge way off, and you plan to use those two retail prices as your "bone" strikes to enforce an iron condor.

Around the same moment, you are selling to open a 25-strike place, biding around $0.15, and buying to raise the 24-strike put, requested at $0.06. You immediately offer about the other part of a condor to enable a 27-strike request, offered at $0.13 and purchase to activate the 28-strike request, requested at $0.03. You received $0.28 on a couple of options offered, then paid $0.09 on the options bought, with a total profit of $0.16 ($0.28-$ 0.09). Upon joining the pool, multiplying the initial compensation by 100 ordinary shares per deal, you have earned $19.

Potential Iron Condor Benefit and Breakeven Rails

The target is for XYZ stocks to live over the duration of the options in between sold 25 and 27 hits, and you can keep the full $19 bonus. Yet as far as the stock stays around two break-even point rails — the sell call strike and net payment ($27.19) and the sell put hit minus net compensation ($24.81) — your iron condor should be profitable.

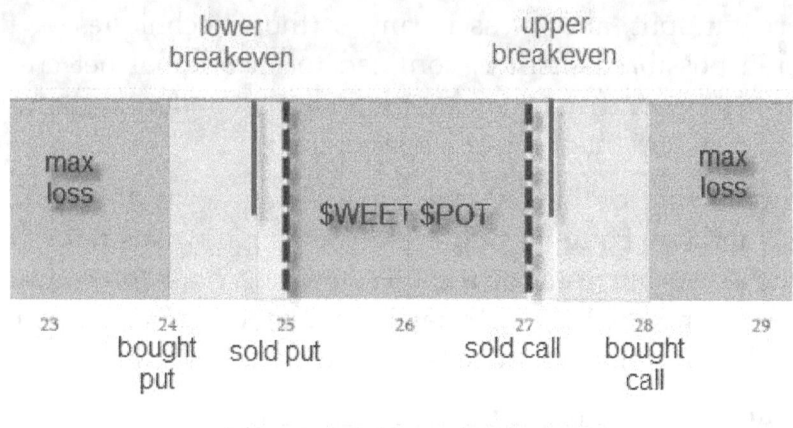

The risk of Iron Condor is limited but can be substantial.

Because every one of them sold options at a near strike is shielded by a bought option, future losses through an iron condor are minimal. If XYZ will spike above $28 — the bought call strike price — the amount you will risk is restricted to the gap between the purchased and selling call strikes, minus the total credit.

Comparably, if XYZ goes below $24 — the put strike bought — the more you will lose equal to the gap between the put strikes bought and exchanged, the fewer the net credit — again, [(25-24) -$0.19] equals to $0.81, or $81.

After all, if some of your sold possibilities move into the money before expiry, you might want to purchase to shut down the agreement to prevent assignment — incur an extra service charge.

3 Things to consider until an Iron Condor is implemented

1. Bet on stocks that you anticipate to stay within a small range, and pick options that hit appropriately. Over the last year, stocks with weak Schaeffer's Risk scoreboard (SVS) levels have continued to allow undermanned changes on the board, compared to what the sector in options has traded in.

2. Try to focus on short-term options, and there's less scope for the residual market to turn toward you. So, ensure that there are no possible securities-moving motivators until expiries, such as an income deadline or a significant event.

3. Be mindful, however, that an iron condor needs four starting transfers, which converts into far higher brokering expenditures than the two-legged payment set. Weigh the entrance fee against someone's big benefit.

Chapter 12: Set the passive profits by trading options

Making inactive earnings online during the day trading in 2020 may exactly look like a dream. But can it become truth, too? The discrepancies between passive and active earnings should first be discussed to address the issue. Then we'll look for how to produce passive revenue by different investment strategies, like securities, bitcoin, forex, and much more.

Reactive income is generated regularly with money requiring minimal action on behalf of the beneficiary to earn as well as maintain it. The kinds of earnings that spring to mind are also returns on securities, debt, assets, earned wages, and investment income.

Although the latter does suit the common concept of passive revenue, certain countries do enforce a more specific interpretation for taxation purposes. The complexities underlying these tax decisions are more discussed below.

Passive Vs. Active Trading

Active Trading

Users also wonder whether investment investing represents passive profits. The response, however, would rely on your approach individually. Effective investors would invest great time and energy into making money. In reality, their trading operation is always the key focus of their activities.

Passive Trading

So, although, if you're trying to produce a passive profit from the day investing, you 're not necessarily going to waste the entire day watching the stocks and conducting business at your home. Like aggressive traders, instead of dictating your life, the passive revenue should work perfectly.

So, for instance, if you'd like to produce passive revenue from option or bitcoin investing, you might want to turn over your money to a trustworthy trader, automation network, or invest by copy investing.

How to develop Passive Income

Automation

Some switch to automation to allow daytime trading of passive profits. Automated programs can help you produce significant income when employed correctly. It is just because there are just a handful of trades that you can perform manually every day. Whereas when predefined conditions have been achieved, a complex algorithm will automatically reach and exit places.

They also allow you to trade simultaneously in a lot of stores. In reality, if you've configured the parameters, when you're asleep, you can produce passive income.

Some will question the usefulness of such schemes, understandably. About 75% of every trade made mostly on the London stock exchange, as well as the NASDAQ, now come from these methodologies, displaying their capacities.

Software

You'll have to find the appropriate tools until you can start building an additional income from automatic stock trading, for instance. Check your ratings and do your homework before you participate in some.

Once you've settled on a platform, you'll need a successful plan to create. Often a good way to continue is to build a list of your whole trading criteria. Perhaps you'd like to consider:

- On reaching and leaving places
- Match role
- Calendar intraday trading

- Goals and stop-losses

Back-Testing

Of starters, until you can get an automatic program to produce a passive revenue from bitcoin, you'll actually have to back test the plan. This gives you the opportunity to test the system before risking any capital. To get a gauge on how beautiful it performs, you literally run your device toward historical price data. Then, you can identify and fix any problems.

The simulation on Monte Carlo is a helpful gadget to try. It checks the algorithm moves frequently and inserts random numbers into the parameters. It will enable you to predict how good your latest program will do.

Application

Thankfully finished with working hard, you might now start seeing passive revenue mount up in the portfolio. You do need to test the program performs regularly as planned, however. There may be technological malfunctions and irregularities.

Algorithm

You'll have to get the equation published after you've built a plan. You will be allowed to penetrate guidance yourselves if you've any technical skills because the coding is fairly easy. If not, however, you might want to try recruiting a developer for help.

Pros & Cons of Passive Income

Until we look at any strategies and suggestions to gain passive day income investing, it is crucial that you consider the advantages as well as the disadvantages. One immediate advantage is the small number of resources you will have to commit. However, that also ensures that the investment choices you make are placed under added scrutiny.

Furthermore, active trading may also result in a low-income stream when contrasted with stock investing. There's also a danger of you neglecting to monitor your additional income. It can lead to losses in future income. Conversely, you can waste too much time stressing over your roles that you can intervene unnecessarily, restricting returns.

Copy Trading

Arguably, one way to make it convenient to sell passive profits is by selling versions. You will gain from its performance of seasoned merchants, instead of devoting enormous energy and time to designing a plan and tracking the stocks.

You simply pick a trader, but then a designed trader can simulate purchase and sell the trader with your money. Nonetheless, you can also encounter the vendors, so a limited amount of the income will be taken from the platform. Indeed, those who replicate investors can then also be replicated and commissions awarded.

Drawbacks

You may think this is the perfect way to start investing in forex as an investment income. Even so, whether it's stocks, options or forex, certain pitfalls tend to be considered:

• Venture capital – You have to be willing to risk all the money you originally spent owing to market uncertainty. If you're especially risk-averse, having a few days of major losses can also stop you from sleeping.

• Trader selection – Choosing a trader is also no simple challenge. A violent crypto trader, for example, could clear everyone out in a few days. Find their preference and approach tool, then. Check out their recent history of trade, too. You want outcomes that are smooth and constant. However, it's worth remembering that several individuals may consider some seasoned traders to clone.

- Not Proportionally following transactions – Certain places cannot require you to exchange substantially. However, traders also spend particular sums, for fair, if not simple purposes. So, make sure that you really hang to replicating your seller.

- Learning method vs. promised money maker – Many claims that trade duplication is better used by newcomers as a resource to learn about various markets and tools. So, keep in mind it might not be the best way to generate a day-long passive income exchange.

Overall, you might also want to take into account both of the above methods for those involved in day-trading for unearned income. Each could considerably lower the value of time people need to trade in intraday. It is also important to note, however, that they come with inconveniences and threats. The task, though, is to determine which best fits the particular lifestyle and needs.

Taxes and passive income

Trading is the correct way for you all to generate passive jobs before you make a decision day; other rules and regulations were also worth considering. Many taxation policies split income sources into three categories:

- Passive – also called net operating revenue and profit from an activity in which the investor is not directly active. It may also provide value that is paid to itself. That definition includes a range of causalities. You don't have to be overly interested in the intraday trading practices to slip into that category.

- Fund – Equity and asset investment capital returns, such as bonds, commodities, oil, ETFs, etc., are usually called fund profits. It may have or may not be called passive profits, though.

- Effective – because, as the name implies, you will engage yourself actively and significantly in the company. For example, if you are to spend much of the day making intraday trade, you might fall into that group.

Such meanings change when you switch through various tax jurisdictions, to some degree. However, the argument is that it is prudent to test which form of a trading operation is going to constitute additional income wherever you stay, plus that you ought to be mindful of some specific tax regulations.

Just like non-passive profits, several countries make passive income tax as well. It may also be handled differently, as well. For e.g., across the Us, the IRS lets to write off passive losses only over passive profits. And, if profits outweigh profit from discretionary day trading operations, the majority of the loss will be rolled over to the following tax year as soon as there is a taxable income from which to pay it off.

Passive profit is of necessity what most people like. Why wouldn't you want the opportunity to raise money while you have a nice night out? Traditionally, however, day-trading was viewed as an aggressive, duration-consuming way of producing income.

Fortunately, digital technology today, to some degree, enables individuals to have a previous seat and yet deliver income. However, you will find a program that fits the particular situation, thus considering the uncertainties and any tax laws into account.

Chapter 13: Options case study- relationship between underlying assets and options

To research the dynamic existence and relationships of the options with the fundamental asset, we offer a case research of options. Learning its use or payments of possibilities will be much simpler and we'll see it throughout practice. However, first let us examine briefly the features of the different key alternatives.

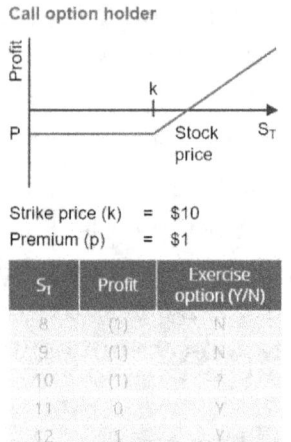

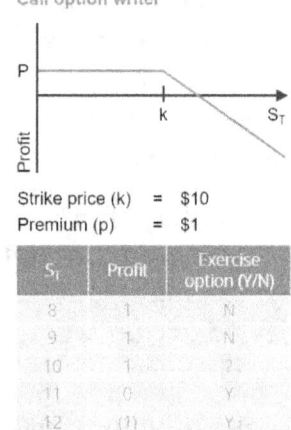

Case Study Options: Definitions

A choice is an acquired derivatives contract, for the most part with the actual asset. The choice contract offers the investor the right to buy or resell the tradition offers at a fixed price from or return to the choice owner. The issuer of the right is not obliged to match the offer, and will cause it to expire if trading conditions were not lucrative for exercising.

They all come with both the following options:

- **Pries for strike**

- **Full volume**

The market rate is the asset value price over which an option manager may exercise the right of purchasing or selling a defined sum of an underlying commodity. The quantity is the sum of an underlying securities to be exchanged after option exercise.

Tools may be either American or British alternatives, too. The adjectives are not linked to the area of the option (it is possible to buy a U.S option at an Asian return). Briefly, until and up to the expiry, an American alternative is exercisable. Only after expiry is a European right exercisable.

Put Option

An option contract is the correct decision for the owners of the contract to offer or "transfer" the commodity money into the economy. In return for the market price the option put gets x sum of the stock. The cost of a put option increases as the price of the asset's commodity falls below the price of the right hit. It is just because an option investor will now offer the product at a premium greater than the prevailing market level.

Call Option

The choice buyer has the money to access the commodity in a call contract. The alternative is so-called since it helps the owner to "dial" the resource. The owners of the right must buy the negotiated sum of the commodity at a strike point. If the valuation of an underlying commodity decreases to an above the option's strike price, a short call grows in valuation. That is since the contract also offers the buyer the opportunity to buy the commodity at a price that is cheaper than the actual market value.

Moneyness

Options often have a Money feature. When a market price on each type of choice is equal to the specified price, it is recognized as the money. In the wealth option is recognized as an alternative with just a market price in which activity would be financially viable. Conversely, if practiced, the out of that money decision would lead to a loss.

Options Case Study Proper

Let us look at the scenario of a company that worried about the high prices of the particular input. To keep things convenient, we are discussing the rising oil prices of the plastic creator concerned. The price already sits at 25 dollars a tank. A company fears that the market will climb above $30 for each barrel.

A manufacturing company will buy a margin call at $30 for every barrel to resolve that issue. The covered call market rate is proportional to the maker's expectations of the expected level.

Options Case Study Transactions

The producer (the right holder) charges the choice writer a fee on purchasing of the call contract. The prices are governed by the stock market, but are impacted on the agreed price by a target price or volume.

If the price never reaches $30 a tank, the right would run out of liquidity. The producer wasn't at a major disadvantage, though, because they will cause the right to expire and just buy the crude oil below the level of $30. The risk on the right (excluding planned oil buying gains / risk) is literally the prime charged to the publisher.

If the price settles down at $30 a barrel and holds unchanged, otherwise the capital right disappears. The holder choice can claim the option, or cause it to expire. That is subjective, as the producer would buy oil at $30, anyway. The risk mostly on option here is always clearly the prime charged to the artist.

After all, if the price reaches $30 a tank, the right runs out of the pocket. The manager right begins making a return on the contract. For instance, if the industry is at $33 the company will work out the alternative and buy the writer's oil at $30 for each barrel. The right investor earns a return from the fee charged out of their investments. If the price is $1, then in this scenario, the revenue is $2. This can be reached by ($33-$ 30)-$ 1. They are also safe from oil costs exceeding $30, as their choice gains would at least partly defray the increased buying cost of oil.

The call choice is used, in our case, as a protection over the oil price. The call choice relationship is the same independently of the sector. In our instance, we view and the out -of- the wealth option restricts the disadvantages to the price charged also on option for a plastic supplier. For all consumer rates up to or including market price and premium there is the drawback. If the selling price crosses a strike price + premium, though, the producer continues profiting. This / upside income is infinite.

In short, the plastic producer is hedging effectively toward a predicted increase in fuel prices. Buying a call choice restricts risk to high price but does not tie upside down, leaving it unrestricted.

Chapter 14: Greeks method

Greeks are also used to calculate the numerous factors which affect the value of a choice. This included Delta, Theta, Gamma, Rho and Vega. We're not going to go into Rho though, as it only tests how responsive an alternative is to inflation rate shifts. This is normally not a major consideration, and is generally only noticed as interest rate increases. What you need to note is that Rho calculates the potential variance in the price of a choice per 1 percent change in risk-free zone.

(Theta and Vega)

The successive Greek is Vega. this identify the variation of the cost of an option for a one-day fall in its expiry time. Theta lets you reduce the price of a contract when the choice is nearing expiry. Your biggest opponent is theta, or period fall, while you're long choices. At the other side, theta is the best buddy if you are lacking choices.

Options lose interest when their maturity approaches; if all other conditions stay the same, theta calculates how much interest the choice would lose per day.

Because options are non-linear, the ATM theta usually decreases when expiration reaches just marginally OTM and ITM choices. In the other side, as exhaustion progresses, theta of extreme out: of-the-money option typically declines.

If you glance at the sequence of choices again you can see the values of theta.

If you search at the ATM possibilities, or calls or puts for $190 market price, theta seems to be -0.15. This ensures the options will sacrifice $0.15 in interest when each week passes, despite all else becoming equivalent. This might be useful when considering options to theoretically sell.

Vega

Vega is not really a Greek alphabet but understanding is still essential. Vega calculates the rate of improvement in the price of an option with each 1 per cent increase in the corresponding stock's high vol. Essentially it informs you how much the price of an option should be moving when the underlying safety or index volatility goes up or down.

Vega measures why a stock's volatility affects the options prices on another stock. For starters, take a glance at this Fb Inc. (FB) options chain of Greeks.

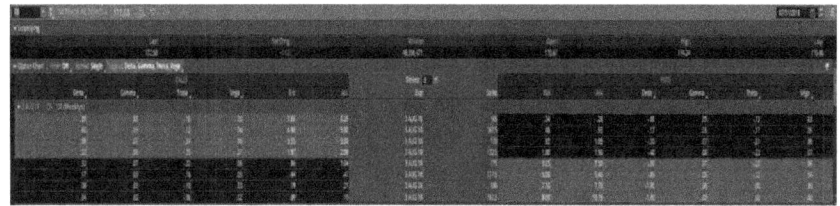

Let's look at a call & puts for a $172.50 market price. Since FB traded about $172.50, those would be at-the-money. The calls and the puts have 0.07 Vega. Which implies that the options will vary by $0.07 with every 1 per cent increase in the amount of high vol.

If you ignore Vega, purchasing options could theoretically "overpay." All things being same, you will suggest purchasing options while deciding strategy while Vega is below "usual" levels or selling options if Vega is above "standard" rates. Yet another way to assess that is to start comparing the implied data with the volatility implied. Most platforms of options let you do this.

Typically, a reduction in Vega will result in both calls and loss of value. In the other side, Vega's growth usually pushes calls rates and brings them higher.

Now you must have a clear knowledge of the Greeks. You'll have to study it again and again for it to become really intuitive, though. In fact, if you have exposure to a network of alternatives, this is much easier.

(Delta and Gamma)

Delta

Delta evaluates how much of the value of an option in the company's securities is prepared to vary per each $1 move. We've expanded on this before.

Call choices have a favorable variance and range between 0 and 1. The at-the-money plans usually have deltas near 0.50. When you look at the adjustments in the options, the further you get into the capital, the greater the delta. A delta will approach to deep within the cash segment 1. In addition, as we reach the expiry date, the money call possibilities delta will be approaching $1. It acts more or less like a portfolio, when an option becomes deeper in the pocket. At the other side, when we reach the end date, opportunities for out: of-the-money calling hit zero.

Put options get a pessimistic variance on the flip-side, varying from -1 to 0. In fact, just speak of what we said of call choices, but with pessimistic values. Typically, in-the-cash call options get a delta close to -0.50 As the money option deepens, delta reaches -1. When we move more out of the market and near termination, certain options' delta reaches 0.

Here's a look at AAPL 's chain of options shown with the Greeks. Apple was priced about $190 so you could easily see how the difference shifts as you glance at the strike rates. The $200 contract price contracts have a 0.23 delta although the $182.50 contract price contracts have a 0.70 delta. The $200 contract price puts get a delta of -0.77 on the flip side whereas the $182.50 market price starts to put get a delta of -0.28.

Gamma

The Greek next is gamma. For every $1 variance in an underlying stock, Gamma calculate the responsiveness of a delta option. Essentially, gamma means you decide how much the delta of an option ought to change as fundamental stock prices.

One reason to mention about delta, it is just a snapshot. It is accurate at a given time and price only. The Delta adjusts as a margin requirement shifts. Because delta cannot surpass -1 and +1, gamma reduces as the right in the money gets higher.

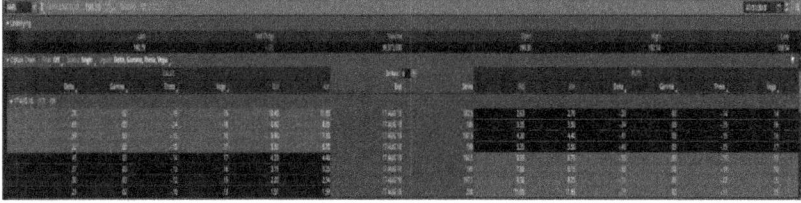

The $182.50 fixed price calls get a gamma with 0.03 when you take a gander at the possibilities string on AAPL.

That means the delta will be chaining by 0.02 per each $1 transformation in the share price.

Chapter 15: Other important factors for options

Options Pricing

There are a number of choices out there to price types. Pricing of options is, however, a path in itself. You'll want a lot of math and a little physics to grasp the concept behind pricing options. Don't be afraid though. Here we'll concentrate on the fundamentals and aim at a factor influencing the value of an option.

Now there are 3 major factors influencing the price of stock options:

- Price on the stock market
- Deadline to close
- Volatilities

The "less" significant factors that influence the price of options:

- quick-term interest rates
- Shares

Please remember that if they normally changing the asset prices will also matter. Having said that, let's look at how those things influenced the price of an option.

The Substantial Price

For put options, the price of the option should boost whenever the fundamental stock's price increases. When stock fall the reverse is real. But at the other side, as the fundamental demand hikes, it pushes down contract premiums. If the value of the commodity stock increases, choice compensation will increase. Pretty quick right? If people remember earlier you could see clearly how their PnL will also change whenever the price of the stock changes.

Time Value and Expiration

If there's a huge amount of time available before the expiry date of the contract, the price will be greater. In other terms, a six-month contract up to the expiry date will also have a great cost than one of one month before expiry, all the rest being equivalent.

Volatility

Uncertainty is the tendency propensity vary in price for the company's securities. That means uncertainty represents the magnitude of the change in price and has no bias in one way or another toward price action. You have to realize the greater volatility, the greater the premium option should be. The less liquidity, the less prime.

Interest Rates

Interest rates generally have no effect on premium costs more than the opportunity cost, the fundamental share price, but also volatility. If interest rates, though, undergo a large degree of volatility, then prices matter. A rise in interests' rates usually raises calling prices and, based on the popular Black-Scholes price formula, lowers put prices. This concept has drawbacks so it's an industry norm. We 're not going to get into those specifics of such a pricing model however.

Dividends

Shares are also sold on condition that they are only performed on an expiry date. That ensures that if a stock releases a dividend, a call options will be sold for the same value as the earnings. Holding options will be more costly, though, as the market price would decrease by the value of the dividend just after payment of dividends.

Such considerations should be well known before you pass forward, and how they impact choice rates. Next, we should look at an increasingly critical subject: the intrinsic and the extrinsic meaning.

Intrinsic Value vs. Extrinsic Value

The value of an option consists of two main components: the inherent and the extrinsic utility.

An inherent value basically informs us how much an option will be valued when contrasted with the volatility of the asset stock and the price of the shot. Let's use the example from above in Apple (AAPL). Apple was priced about $200 or assuming you've bought 1 demand choice that expires in two weeks. An option offers you the opportunity to $200 to purchase the order. Assume Apple went to $210, so there is already a week to go before the expiry date. Said that, normally at $10, or $1,000, must be worth your pick.

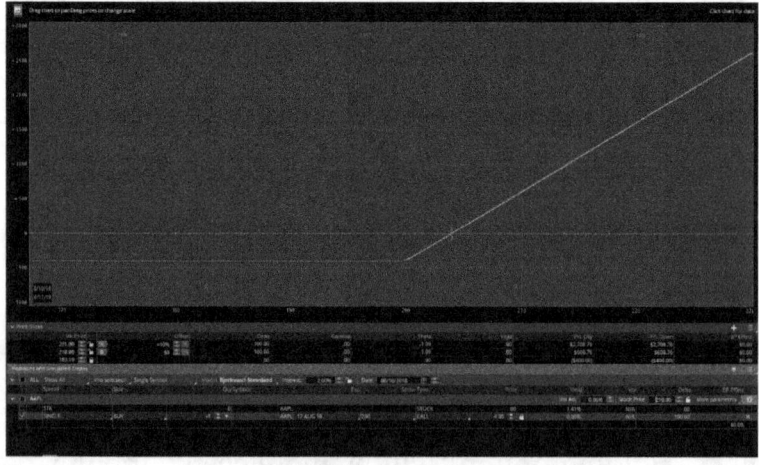

As you can see, your PnL was $608 when the inventory was trying to trade at $210, so the options have been good enough to justify $1,000 (the premium amount paid).

If the put options were trying to trade under $10, traders could buy the call, exercise this same call request buy the stock immediately below the existing trading price for a net price. This is regarded as risk-free volatility benefit and, at happen for a long time, cannot occur on the market.

Arbitrators usually eat those earnings before they even get an opportunity to do anything.

Now, when an option has not yet expired it has extrinsic value as well. The derivative market is the component of an option value which represents the fact that the choice is optional. Let's start with our example of an AAPL alternative, for example. If AAPL trade at $200, there is no inherent interest to the $195 long positions. You certainly don't want to pursue the possibility of selling AAPL stock at $195 while traded at $200, that's a risk for the moment. If the puts get enough time before their expiration date, however, it may still have any worth. It is because there is a chance that AAPL will be priced around $195. The puts became in-the-money and get an inherent value of $10 if the stock falls to $190.

Out-of-the-money, In-the-money, and on-the-money just represent the moneyness of an opportunity in relation to the price of the hit. For e.g., if a stock trad at $20, a $15 contract price putt options will be labeled outside of-the-money, whereas the $25 contract price call options will be labeled out-of-the-money. In comparison, the call or put options of $20 will be called at-the-money.

Said that, the external value represents the benefit of owning the right as in the future the inherent value will increase.

This puts out to consistency with the put-call.

Dimensional trading

Different Ways to Use Options

The elegance of choices is a fact that Trading allows users to be innovative. Options are among the most competitive asset groups on the sector, since the trading opinion can be correctly mirrored. You can purchase a long position, purchase a bull spreads or purchase the common assets and protect with long positions, whether you're bullish. If you're bearish, on the other side, you might purchase a call options, distribute a bear or shorten the common assets and protect to put options. You might purchase a straddle if you don't know whether a stock would go up or down so you assume it will go a ton in any direction. The options are limitless. Don't panic if you don't learn the lingo of various tactics for choices yet, during the upcoming section we'll go through this in depth.

Having said that, let 's look at a certain various way of using options.

Directional Options Trading

Options can be used to generate exposure to fundamental stock prices. It is defined as positional options trading and speculating is something a lot of buyers do. The easiest method to use the products is either to purchase a margin call or even a put alternative. When you're optimistic you should purchase a call choice, like we mentioned earlier. Alternatively, you 'd purchase a put option if you're bearish.

For e.g., let 's say you see Square (SQ), so when it was selling at $70, you figured it might go up to $80. You might purchase call options instead of purchasing the stock directly, or write call options.

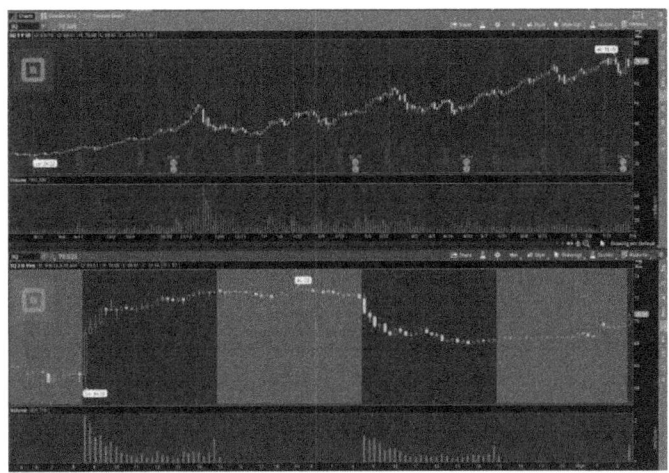

Here's a look at the Chain of Options.

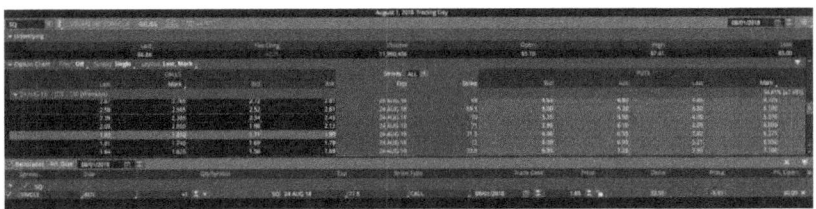

Let's say you purchase the call option 1 SQ 25 AUG 17 $71.50 and bill $1.85. If a stock will move to $80 somewhere on the expiry date, the right will be apparently worth $8.50.

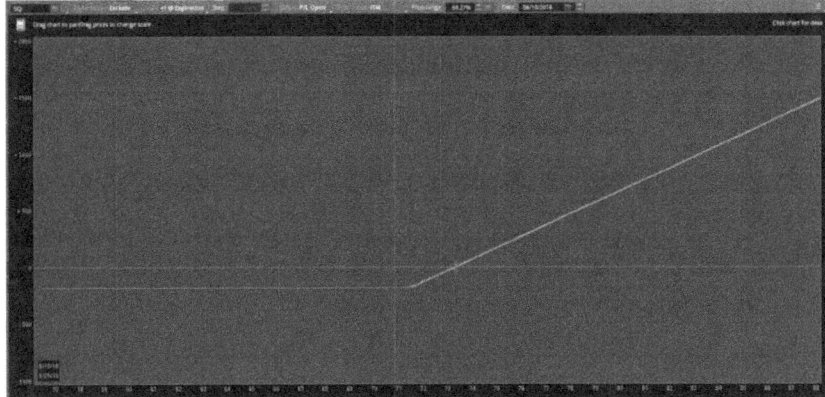

Writing puts or calls would be some other way of expressing your bearish viewpoints, respectively. These are incredibly dangerous now and we're not suggesting that newcomers go outside or write options. We can't stress enough how, you get a high level of risk when you're writing naked, or short choices. How if you compose put options on a portfolio when you're highly optimistic, but the business goes bankrupt? Yeah, those put rights will be very costly and you're going to have to sell the securities to eventually have a margin offer. You not want to have a margin call anyway as that means you don't run your company properly.

Let's presume another trader on SQ is bearish, so he doesn't think he will live above $70.

Unless the stock climbs to $80, a certain trader might be in a painful 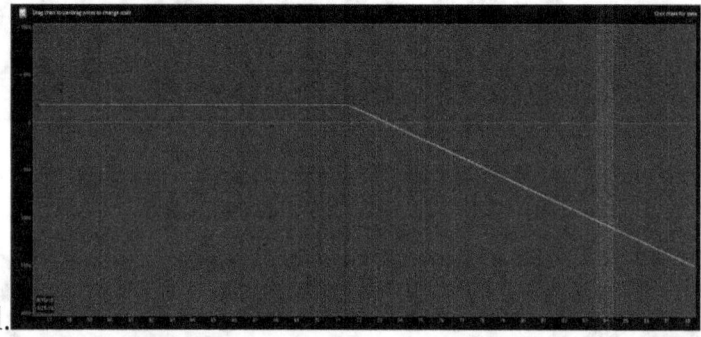 world.

You see, you don't ever know how much a stock can move from here. So, ability to write options without really being hedged is highly hazardous and when you first learn to trade options, you should move away from it.

Writing Options to Generate Income

You can also compose choices for collecting premiums or generating income, note.

Personally, I don't believe this is good for traders beginning options because if you're not hedged it's extremely risky but it's worth going through. Additionally, if their short options role doesn't work out you don't want to pull up your credit card.

This approach is based on the fact that certain options possess extrinsic value, that will be discounted by the moment the options end. So, the concept here is that the fall in worth, also known as linear decay, or theta decomposition, might be collected for a profit by selling options. Even if the extrinsic value falls as the option approaches its expiration, as well as intellect, date, the inherent value may still rise.

Let's take an example by feel. Here we're going to go over call option strategy. A call option strategy consists of a broad stock position or a short call.

So, if you own a portfolio, trying to sell out-of-the-money put options on the company's securities might raise your returns. You'd lose money if the stock falls, but the calls would mature worthlessly and you'd mitigate the profits because you've earned the premium. Here is for examples a glance at a covered call technique.

Take this example SQ. Suppose you're 100 stock shares long, but don't think it can get more than $75.

You are selling a call option 1 SQ $100 24 AUG 18, and you're big from $66.

On a flip side, unless the inventory rallies as well as keeps making highs, you 'd benefit from the stock's rise in value. You 'd lose money at the short position though. Theoretically a covered call has infinite reward value as forecasting where a stock will go is almost impossible. Since you're hedged only with situation, if you're exercised on such options, you 'd still be profiting, which would have been comparable to the call option's strike price less the stock purchase price. Here is a traffic off. What about if the inventory is up 40 percent in buyout negotiations, then the positive side is restricted? If the product starts falling below the mark, the maximum loss will be reduced to the amount you pay for the stock minus the bonus you got.

Conclusion

This guideline offers you the full description on why choose options? We've attempted to address the query using concrete examples and ideally, you're beginning to become familiar with the concept of including options in your everyday routine investment. Options open up other possibilities; possibilities for leveraged lending, prudent sales production, and equity protection as well. So why is it that choices are always deemed more expensive than inventories? Of course, the gap is time. Since options sometimes expire worthlessly, you may potentially lose your whole investment. That's why it's crucial to consider both the danger and possible benefits of every option trade before you join it, and the technology today currently enables any investor, private or experienced, to analyze a potential option trade with unprecedented pace and apparent simplicity.

Computer program that models option trading actions may be of considerable benefit. Trading opportunities are completely feasible without the help of machines and financial tools. But why would you be in such a disadvantage when you are in? Software for the analysis of options performs all the measurements for you, and exhibits risk graphs that allow you to make essential trade decisions quickly. There is a major benefit in graphically displaying all possible consequences, including how a position would react to market price shift, time decrease, and implied volatility shifts. Certainly, it would be seen by the citizens you transact against. Trading options efficiently can sometimes be difficult, even with the proper tools; why intentionally attempt to make it tougher?

One of the major differences among options and inventories is that options are really agreements. They have always had two sides so there's someone else selling it for every visit or put purchased. It's a zero-sum game. That implies a buyer benefit option is the loss of the seller alternative, or vice versa. Just because of that, the smaller version of the seller's profit and loss profile must be any payout representation of the USD returns from buying a choice.

A need to vigilance

Maybe the toughest thing of buying and selling products is self-discipline. If you ever don't set your own policy and trading rules about when to close trades, how to reduce risks, or just what you're hoping to achieve, otherwise trading options will be hard to

take advantage of. The good options trader is someone who recognizes the power of self-discipline but has the opportunity to enter and close positions according to predetermined trading rules, just because you're inclined to do otherwise. The rapidly changing complexity of the stock market, ever-looming expiry dates and the numerous factors affecting an option's time value all allow you to be mindful of how time functions for or against you to increase your earnings.

Two Policies

There are two wide areas where you need to develop policies: first, know why you use alternatives, and secondly, know your escape point!

Initially, consider what your option trading aim is. Would you use leveraged trading options? If so, you 'd best have the correct market forecasting resources to cause successful entries and exits.

Using options to generate money from your portfolio holdings? So, realize which of those shares have stocks with high rates of implied volatility to make the sale opportunity worth the trouble. Eventually, you could use the options as investment loss insurance. If so, imagine the collar technique utilized every day by countless organizations. In brief, consider the option trader label in which you come.

A unique escape plan is included in the second policy area. You need to worry of future situations and determine when to close a place — in advance. You will keep options before the day of expiry or abandon the week before. If you buy an opportunity, you would define a sale point for benefit as well as a turnaround point for losses. You can want to sell when you make your money (upside down) or lose one-third (upside down). Laws like this, irrespective of what the particular escape points are, describe a specific occurrence where intervention is needed.

Exposure of threats is just another thing to remember. Let's assume, for instance, your short calls and the expiry day is close. The stock itself is level out of the market and now just 10 cents worth the option. Can you wait for an expiration and take the chance that the stock will leap until the option expires, given that the choice is near to the money? This might be sensible to just close the position for a dime per agreement, just in scenario the stock rose at the last minute.

You'll more definitely excel if you obey the laws and avoid the urge to make exceptions. No criteria to get out at the correct moment, undoubtedly you will crash. Neither shares nor options may be considered as separate components of the fund. They will co-operate. That is the value of options: As part of the overall investing plan, they are valuable.

The Next Steps

Where to go from here? You must proceed your teaching and start assembling the tools you need to trad. Books, seminars, alternative trading courses and directories of expert choices all have a place in the trading education. Yet trading is nowadays almost impossible without connection to a device, including tools to monitor transactions to get current market details. Your personal finance does not target at achieving a certain level. So, it's a process and even the most seasoned traders have to keep contributing to their awareness of investing. Try always having a broker who is experienced in options. At the significant brokerage firms, you can trade choices in certain equity accounts (with some extra documentation and an assertion stating you assess the dangers linked with options), but options-specific firms can also provide you with skills and information that will assist you in your trade.

The pillars we described in this guide expand on all option trades. Keep in mind to take your time to consider when to trade an option, or to understand a common spread trade. Trading paper (without jeopardizing actual money) is one way to start acquiring knowledge and understanding how options are having. When you learn the options principles and tactics, you will be performing great before you finally start trading them. Enjoy the obstacles, the incentives and the road!

References

Why Spreads Matter. Retrieved, from
https://www.investopedia.com/terms/s/spread.asp

Rallies, T., Around, C., Thinks, A., Stagflation! T., Bonds, T., & 'U'?, I. Use Technical Analysis to Determine Your Best Option Spread Trading Strategy | Stock Investor. Retrieved from https://www.stockinvestor.com/27475/use-technical-analysis-determine-best-option-spread-trading-strategy/

Trading Technical Analysis . Retrieved, from
https://tradingsim.com/blog/understanding-options-with-technical-analysis/

How to Choose an Online Stock Broker. Retrieved from
https://www.investopedia.com/investing/complete-guide-choosing-online-stock-broker/

Top 10 Option Trading Mistakes: Watch How to Trade Smarter Now, from

https://www.ally.com/do-it-right/investing/top-10-option-trading-mistakes/

What is a Bull and a Bear Market? – Money Instructor. , from
http://content.moneyinstructor.com/693/what-bull-bear-market.html

How to Think Like a Trader - Winning Mindset of a Master Traders, from https://corporatefinanceinstitute.com/resources/knowledge/trading-investing/winning-mindset-of-a-trader/

3 Ways to Combat Forex Trading Anxiety & Build Confidence, from

https://www.learntotrade.co.za/3-ways-to-combat-trading-anxiety/

How Investing With LEAPS Could Generate Huge Returns. from

https://www.thebalance.com/using-leaps-instead-of-stock-to-generate-huge-returns-358082

How Investing With LEAPS Could Generate Huge Returns. From **https://www.thebalance.com/using-leaps-instead-of-stock-to-generate-huge-returns-358082**

Options Strategies in Low Volatility Environment - Weekly Money Multiplier, from **https://www.weeklymoneymultiplier.com/options-trading-strategies-low-volatility/**

www.ingramcontent.com/pod-product-compliance
Lightning Source LLC
Chambersburg PA
CBHW071401210526
45465CB00001B/201